Gloucestershire
Folk Tales
for
Children

Gloucestershire
Folk Tales
for
Children

Anthony Nanson and Kirsty Hartsiotis

The History Press

First published 2020

The History Press
97 St George's Place, Cheltenham,
Gloucestershire, GL50 3QB
www.thehistorypress.co.uk

British Library Cataloguing in Publication Data.
A catalogue record for this book is available from the British Library.

ISBN 978 0 7509 9136 0

Typesetting and origination by The History Press
Printed and bound in Great Britain by TJ International Ltd.

CONTENTS

THINGS YOU CAN DO WITH THESE STORIES

The first thing to do, of course, is *read* the stories! We hope you enjoy them. You may want to read them aloud to your family or friends. If you don't enjoy reading aloud, get someone else to do the reading so you can enjoy listening. Read one story at one time, another story another time. Now and again you may see an unusual spelling where a character is speaking Gloucestershire dialect.

Why have we called these stories 'folk tales'? 'Folk' means the stories come from the ordinary *folk* of Gloucestershire or have to do with their customs. 'Tales' means stories that are *told*. What's the difference between *telling* and *reading*? When you *read* a story, you have the book in front of you and you read out the exact words. When you *tell* a tale, you don't have any text; you just tell the story from memory. There's no need to learn by heart the exact words in the book. Forget about that! All you have to remember is the gist of the story – the main things that happen. When you tell the story, you can use whatever words you want. The words will be different each time you tell the same tale!

Sometimes people think that telling a story like this must be difficult. It isn't really. We think that telling a story is more fun than reading it, but then we would – we're storytellers! The important thing is to remember the main things that happen in the story. It's useful to make a list of these. Even better is to make a 'storyboard'. That's just a posh word for a comic strip. Take a big sheet of paper and divide it up into, say, eight

boxes. In each of the boxes draw a picture of one of the important events in the story you want to tell. Make sure you put them in the right order! Underneath each picture you could write a few words to sum up what's happening. A storyboard is a nice thing to make, but it's also a handy tool to remind you of the gist of the story.

Now you should be ready to tell the story to some of your family or friends. A younger brother or sister can be a good audience! It's best to put away the storyboard before you tell the story, so you and your audience can focus on telling and listening.

When you tell one of the stories, you may find that it changes quite a bit. That's absolutely fine. Stories are always changing. If you enjoy writing, you may want to write your own version of the story. That really gives you the chance to think about how to change the story to make it more interesting to you. If you enjoy drawing and painting, you might want to create a picture of your favourite moment in a story.

If you like acting, then get some friends together to perform a play based on the story. You'll have to decide who is going

to be which characters. Depending on numbers, some actors may need to play more than one character – or even use their bodies to represent the scenery (trees, buildings, etc.). Then you can invite your mum, dad, gran, etc. to come and be the audience. You may need to move some furniture to make enough space. Maybe the furniture – and perhaps some blankets draped over it – can help to provide scenery.

The stories in this book take place in different locations around Gloucestershire. We visited all these places to get a feel for them before we wrote the stories. A brilliant thing to do is ask your mum or dad or guardian to take you to these locations – and then to either tell or read the story right there in the place where it happened. When you do this, the story comes alive in a special way. The place becomes a bit more magical because now it's not just a place but a place with a story. You'll never see those places in the same way again!

While you're there on location why not take some photos or draw a picture of the place? A good project is to keep a scrapbook

in which, on a different page for each story, you stick your photos and drawings and write some words about the places and stories. You could also paste in your storyboards or your own written versions of stories. Or you could do all of this digitally on a blog.

When you've used up the tales in this book, there are lots more stories in other counties of Britain. If you go on holiday in a particular part of the country – or even another country – you could investigate the folk tales there. You'll find books of them in local bookshops or online. Back here in Gloucestershire, maybe when you're a bit older, you can check out the tales in our two other books: *Gloucestershire Folk Tales* and *Gloucestershire Ghost Tales*. Meanwhile, we hope you enjoy this one!

Anthony Nanson and
Kirsty Hartsiotis

MAP OF THE
STORIES

1

GORAM AND VINCENT

Long, long ago, in the mists of time, Britain was inhabited by giants. In the area where, in later times, the city of Bristol was built, there lived two giants. They were brothers. One, called Goram, lived on the Gloucestershire side. The other, Vincent, lived on the Somerset side. Being giants, they were both enormously strong. With their bare hands they could dig and sculpt the bedrock of the land. On Blaise Hill, near Henbury, Goram built himself a gigantic stone chair where he liked to sit with a cup of cider and enjoy the view. On Dundry Down, Vincent

made a triangle-shaped earthwork called
Maes Knoll – and nearby he constructed the
Wansdyke and the stone circle at Stanton
Drew. Vincent really enjoyed digging and
building. He spent most of his time working.

These two brothers, they fell in love with
the same woman. Well, she wasn't really
a woman. She was a giant like them. You
might call her a goddess. Whereas Goram
and Vincent were giants of earth and stone,
Avona was a lady of the water. She gave her
name to her river – the Avon – as smooth
and beautiful as she was. In those far distant
times the Avon pooled to form a huge lake
extending all the way from where Bradford-
on-Avon is today to where Bristol is. Avona
wanted more than anything for her river
to reach the sea. So she said to Goram
and Vincent, 'Whichever of you can dig a
channel to drain the lake, he'll be the one to
whom I'll give my love.'

The two giants both really loved her. They
both felt desperate to be the one who'd drain
the lake. To do that, they'd have to cut through

the limestone hills that blocked the Avon from reaching the Bristol Channel. Goram set to digging a channel right next to his stone chair on Blaise Hill. Vincent began to dig further south near Clifton. They dug and they dug and they dug. It was hot, exhausting work. Goram had a pool – Tarn Lake – where he could wash away the sweat. Beside the pool was a flat-topped rocky stand where he could put his soap – he called it his Soap-Dish. He dug and dug and dug – till he'd cut a steep-sided gorge through the hills. It wasn't quite finished; the gorge would need to go a bit further before it would drain the lake. He was doing well, but he was tired and thirsty. Time to refresh himself with a wash in the pool and then sit on his chair and drink some good Gloucestershire cider. Before he knew it, he'd fallen fast asleep! There he sat in his chair, snoring so loud that the earth vibrated.

Meanwhile, down at Clifton, Vincent was steadily digging away. He loved to dig – and he loved Avona. He just kept digging, pacing his strength, never stopping to rest, though the sweat dripped down his big brawny muscles. He dug and dug and dug – till he'd dug a huge gorge all the way through the hills. As he knocked down the last rocks damming the lake, there was a terrific roar and a torrent of grey water came flooding through, racing in a mad hurry to the sea.

Avona was delighted to see her river flowing so free through this splendid new Avon Gorge. She gave Vincent a big hug and kiss and said she would marry him. Exhausted though he was, Vincent was the happiest giant in Britain.

When Goram woke up, he saw that Vincent's gorge was finished, and much bigger than Goram's, and Vincent had won Avona's love. Goram was furious. 'How could I be so stupid as to fall asleep!' He stamped on the ground – so hard that the earth shook. You can still see the footprint shape of flat bare rock where Goram stamped.

He was so angry that he started being really stupid. He climbed on to the top of his chair and hollered, 'HEY YOU, VINCENT, YOU UGLY GIANT!'

When Vincent heard this shouting, he climbed up to the rocks above his gorge – a spot today called St Vincent Rocks – to see what was going on.

From his vantage point, Goram spotted him. It's hard to miss a giant, even when they're miles away. 'YOU THINK YOU'RE THE BEST, DO YOU?' shouted Goram. 'LET'S HAVE A STONE-THROWING FIGHT AND THEN WE'LL SEE WHO'S THE BEST!'

With that, Goram snapped off a big chunk of rock from the top of his chair and hurled it in the direction of his brother. But the stone was too big and heavy. It fell a long way short – and landed at place today called Druid's Hill. There weren't any druids in the time of the giants, but that big stone was later propped up on three others to make a cromlech, where later still the druids came to pray.

Vincent, having won Avona's love, was feeling much too happy to start throwing stones back at Goram. He climbed back down the cliffs of the gorge and started to dig a cave where he could live close to Avona's river.

That made Goram even more angry. He leapt across the river and began charging around on the Somerset side, shouting at the top of his voice. He sprinted up Dundry Down, looking for things Vincent had made that he could smash up. He was running so fast he wasn't looking where he put his feet. He tripped on the earthwork of Maes Knoll and – because he was moving so fast – went hurtling through the air, far, far through the air, right over Weston-super-Mare, to land with a SPLASH! in the Bristol Channel. There, sad to say, poor Goram drowned. You can still see his head and shoulders jutting above the water as the islands of Steep Holm and Flat Holm.

Vincent was very sad that Goram had drowned. He was his brother, after all. He knew that Goram had lost his temper because he'd loved Avona just as much as Vincent had. He wished that things had worked out differently. Now that Vincent was married to the beautiful Avona, he didn't feel so obsessed with digging and building all the time. Once he'd carved his cave in the cliffs – the Giant's Hole, as it's known – he was content to sit there beside his beloved Avona and watch the river flow below, the tides come and go.

Nowadays there's a bridge across the gorge that Vincent dug, so you can easily cross between the Gloucestershire and Somerset sides. If you go to Henbury and take a walk in the Blaise Castle Estate you can see the smaller gorge that Goram dug and the other things he's left there from that long-ago time: Goram's Chair, Tarn Lake, Goram's Soap-Dish, and the Giant's Footprint where he stamped. As for the stone he threw at Vincent, you can see that in someone's garden on Druid's Hill.

2

THE FAIRY PEEL

It was a topsy-turvy life being a ploughman. For most people working on the farm, the harvest was the busy time. George Greenman of Kingswood was busiest in January. That was when the fields were ploughed so the crops could be sowed. Whereas the harvesters worked in the summer sun, George worked through rain and snow, getting full slabbered with mud. He didn't like it much, but without him and his ploughs there'd be no harvest for anyone.

At Christmastide there was cake to eat and merriment for the two weeks from Christmas Day to Plough Sunday. On that Sunday, George had dressed up in his best and, with the other ploughmen, taken the village ploughs to the church to be blessed by the parson so there would be a good harvest. They'd carried the ploughs through the village afterwards, singing out, 'God Speed the Plough!' There'd been dancing, cider, and a fine meat pudding. But now it was all over and back to work.

Farmer Long had told George to plough one of the fields down by the millstream. George wasn't looking forward to it much. This field had turnips on it last year, and barley the year before that, and would be so claggy that George would have to use his breast plough to work sand into the soil to lighten it. He hated the breast plough. It was nothing but a long spade! With that against your chest, you did all the work yourself. He preferred the plough the oxen pulled – they did half the work for you!

Still, when George looked at the sunlit hills where Wotton-under-Edge nestled, he felt his spirits lift. All morning he worked, listening to the birds singing in the bare trees in the hedge by the brook. He wasn't so happy at lunchtime. His lunch was just crusts, all that was left of his wife's Christmas baking. He thought longingly of the now eaten Christmas cake. Never mind, with the money from this day's work Annie could buy more flour to make more bread.

He'd not long got back to work when a high, shrill cry split the air. The birds stopped singing and George jumped two feet in the air, bouncing the plough right out of the earth. He let it fall and stared wildly around. Into the breathless air the sound came again. A wailing moan of a noise.

There was no one about. The closest building was the mill, but that lay silent today. On the hills to the east he could see Newark Park. George's heart raced as he looked back to the village. He could just see the ruins of the old abbey gatehouse beyond the new church. Everyone knew that a tunnel ran from the abbey to Newark Park and then on through the hill to the Black Quarr Caves. And everyone knew that when Henry VIII had got rid of the monasteries the monks at Kingswood tried to flee through the tunnel. They'd found it blocked and all died down there.

George looked down at the wet soil. Why, the tunnel must run right under his feet! It was ghosts he was hearing, all a-wailing in the bright light of day!

Then, 'Oh no, oh no!' cried the voice. 'My peel is all a-broke!'

Hang on, thought George. That doesn't sound like ghosts! A peel? The long wooden shovel the baker uses to put bread in the oven? Ghosts don't have bread ovens, do they?

The voice broke into sobbing. George had to do something. The voice was coming from the corner of the field where the hedge was thickest and the mud the deepest.

When he got there the sobbing abruptly stopped.

There was nothing to see … Till something bright at his feet caught his eye.

He bent down and – well, there *was* a peel. It was just like the one the baker used, but so tiny only his daughter's doll could have used it. It was broken right in two.

George was a dab hand at mending. When there was no farm work, he often made a penny or two mending folk's tools and furniture. He scooped up the broken peel and slipped it in his pocket.

That evening, when his wife and daughter had gone to bed, he pulled out the two pieces of the peel. It was fiddly work. He smoothed the splintered wood. Cut a little extra wood to make a new handle. A dab of strong glue. The candle had burnt down a couple of marks before he was done.

'As good as new,' he murmured, and slipped the mended peel back into his jacket pocket.

Next morning back at the field, there was still half the ploughing to do, but first George went to the corner where the hedge was thickest. He set down the mended peel and he waited.

There the peel sat while the birds sang and the sun shone.

George shrugged. A good deed was a good deed, even if no thanks were a-coming.

He worked hard that day till the ploughing was done. Tomorrow he'd be working with the oxen on better-drained land. The sun looked set to shine all week. Perhaps his job wasn't *so* bad. But he was hungry. Once more there'd only been crusts for lunch.

As if it were conjured by his thought, he could suddenly smell cake. Rich, fruity cake, well soused in brandy. The smell was coming from the field corner where he'd left the peel.

Heart racing, he clagged back over there, the smell getting stronger with each step.

There, exactly where he'd left the peel, was a tiny fruit cake.

George beamed. 'And I thank ye too.' He bent down to pick up the little cake.

They said you shouldn't eat fairy food, but he was sure this was safe. It was only a morsel – the most delicious cake he'd ever tasted. The taste lingered in his mouth all the way home.

3

THE OWL WAS A BAKER'S DAUGHTER

It was a cold winter's night. Snow was falling thick and fast. Outside, all was silent; no one was to be seen on the streets of the town or on the hills behind it. But inside the bakery on the High Street was warmth and light and busyness. Mrs Povey and her daughter were working furiously to make sure there'd be fresh bread for the town next morning.

It was so hot that young Jenny Povey had to wipe the sweat from her face with her apron. She wasn't used to such hard work. Last year, her dad had been alive; she'd been his pampered pet, treated to sweets and pretty clothes. Now Jenny had to work. It needed two to keep the bakery going, and Mum couldn't afford to hire anyone. Jenny hated the work, but the business would be hers one day, so it had to succeed. She watched every penny that went out and every penny that came in. That night she was chivvying her mum to put the prices up, but Mrs Povey wouldn't do it.

'Got to look after our own, Jenny,' she said. 'Folks'll go hungry if they can't buy bread.'

'Then they should make sure they have enough to buy it,' Jenny cried. 'We're not a charity, you know! We work hard – so they should too!'

Her mum looked at her sadly. Jenny said to herself that things would change when she inherited the bakery. She pounded the dough even harder, feeling very cross, until she was white with flour.

The doorbell rang.

Jenny and her mum jumped and stared at each other wide-eyed. Who could it be at this time of night?

Mrs Povey started towards the door.

'Don't answer it!' said Jenny. 'Nobody's out on honest business on a night like this!'

But her mum was at the door, opening it.

'Aw, Mum!' muttered Jenny as a blast of cold air and snow blew in.

Following the cold air came a man. Jenny had never seen him before. He looked different from their neighbours in the town. His clothes were worn and patched. Her lip began to curl. A beggar! They best send him straight back outside.

'Please, may I have a piece of bread?' said the man.

He had a strange accent. Jenny didn't like that. What was he doing here, in the Cotswolds? She opened her mouth to say no and send him back into the snow.

But Mrs Povey was quicker.

'We're just baking now,' she said. 'You sit yourself down and wait while I pop this in the oven.'

To Jenny's horror, she tore off a huge chunk of risen dough.

'Mum! He doesn't need that much! Come on! Just a little bit will do for the likes of *him*.'

She snatched the dough from her mum, tore off a scrap, and set the rest down. The bit she held was enough for a small bread roll – just right for a layabout like him!

She ignored her mum's protest and thrust the little scrap of dough in the oven. When I'm in charge you won't even get that if you don't pay for it, she thought. He was staring at her, his eyes dark in the lamplight. It made her uncomfortable. She looked away.

Then her mum gasped.

Jenny wheeled around and her eyes nearly popped out of her head.

There was bread oozing out round the door of the oven! How could a little bread roll do that? As she watched, the bread pushed open the oven door and began to bulge into the room. Bigger and bigger it grew. It pushed aside their workbench and stools. Even Jenny's mum was shoved against the wall as the bread swelled out! And now the bread was advancing on Jenny!

She ran for the door, but the man was in the way. She looked again at his bearded face, into his sad eyes. They seemed to hold the weight of the world. He looked strangely familiar now. Where had she seen him before?

'This is all your fault!' she shrieked.

Her mum was crying. Jenny was sure this stupid beggar was doing this. The bread had nearly filled the room! But he was just looking at her sadly.

She got angrier and angrier, and tried to shout something, but the words wouldn't come, so she just screeched – 'Scree, scree, scree!'

She reached out her arms to push the man out the door. She saw then that something strange was happening, not only to the bread but to her as well.

Her arms weren't arms. They were wings! White, floury wings!

She tried to scream, but her mouth wasn't right.

'Scree!' she cried.

Her mouth closed with a click. It had become a beak!

She was turning into a bird! A huge white bird!

The man gave her one last sad look and then he opened the door.

She felt so afraid that she leapt up – and she was flying. As she flew through the doorway she realised where she'd seen him before. In the church, in a painting on the wall – a solemn, bearded, sad-eyed man.

As the snow and cold hit her she knew what she'd done. She'd turned Jesus away and now she was a bird.

On white wings she flew up through the snow, away from the town and into the woods on the hills, screeching into the night.

Jenny Povey never became a girl again. She was an owl for ever, and she was never content. You can still hear her sons and daughters screeching in the night and see them gliding like white ghosts through the air. They couldn't stay away from human places. They've often nested in barns – and they're just as common in church towers, perhaps asking for Jesus' forgiveness.

Today we call them 'barn owls', but in Gloucestershire these owls were once called 'poveys'. Now you know the story why.

4

TO GLOUCESTER A-MOTHERING

It was Lizzie Price's first chance to go home since she started work as a kitchen maid at Painswick Court. Tomorrow was Mothering Day and she wanted to make a simnel cake to take for her mother, but the cook said she wasn't allowed any ingredients from the larder.

Lizzie was so upset. The lady of the house found her crying in the corridor and asked her, 'What's the matter?'

Lizzie told her through her sobs about the cake. She was only thirteen, and a whole year had gone by since she'd last seen her mother.

The lady had no child of her own. She felt sorry for young Lizzie. She took her to the larder and asked her what she needed. Lizzie pointed to the flour, the sugar, the butter, eggs, and fruit.

'Is that all?' asked the lady.

'It's meant to have spices, but I know they be costly.'

'You mustn't make it without spices. You take what it needs.'

'How can I thank you, my lady?'

'You take the cake to your mother. When she gives you her blessing, well, maybe half the blessing will come to me.'

So Lizzie baked her simnel cake. Next morning, she was up before the sun and put on her Sunday best. Everyone in Gloucester would be going to the Cathedral for the Mothering service, so it was there she'd meet her family before they went home for the feast. She wrapped up the cake in a bit of cloth and put it in her basket. She put on her bonnet and shoes and off she went at first light.

At least it had stopped raining. It had rained for days and the roads were a quagmire of mud. Yet spring was in the air. A lively wind tossed the catkins and buds on the branches. The hedgerows were bright with daffodils and celandines, primroses and violets. Other young people were afoot on the roads. Mothering Day was the one day when everyone was freed from their duties to go home to their family and give thanks to God they were halfway through the hardships of Lent. Many of the women were picking armfuls of flowers. Lizzie stopped to pick some too. Only they looked so pretty in the hedgerow, it seemed a shame to pick them. She took just a few, a little bunch for her mother, which she put in her basket.

The first part of the road, climbing round Painswick Beacon, wasn't too wet, but as it snaked down past Upton St Leonards the puddles got bigger and deeper. Holding the basket in one hand, Lizzie tried to lift her skirts with the other. She couldn't stop the bottoms of them dragging in the water. Her shoes were soaked through. She was going to look a sight in the Cathedral!

She noticed then there was no one else about. Where had they all gone?

At a place where there was meant to be a ford across a stream just before the stream joined another, a pool of water had spilled across the road. You couldn't even see the stones of the ford through the murky water. Lizzie lifted her skirts and began to wade through. Soon the water was up to her knees. She went another step and it got deeper yet. She let go of her skirts and lifted the basket high with both hands. Mustn't let the simnel cake get ruined! Her skirts would just have to get wet.

Another step and she sank in deeper – right up to her waist! Would it get even deeper before she reached the other side? The current of the stream was dragging at her skirts. Her arms ached holding up the basket. What was she going to do? There was no one to help. All she could do was pray. So she prayed to Mother Mary. Her master said it was bad to pray to Mary, but it was Mothering Day, the day for mothers and the mother church, so all she could think of was Mother Mary. 'O Mary, Mother of God, please have pity and help me!'

She heard a splash, looked around, and there was a big white horse. The horse had wild wide eyes and her mane was ruffling in the wind. In this bad weather she must have escaped from somewhere. Lizzie trembled as the horse came splashing right up to her, snorting loudly. The horse lowered her head and Lizzie realised what to do. Still clutching the basket with one hand, she reached her other arm round the horse's neck and held on tight as her feet left the ground and the horse dragged her across the flood.

'Thank you,' said Lizzie as the horse trotted on her way.

At least the simnel cake in the basket was still dry. She emptied the water from her shoes, wrung out her skirts, and squelched on down the road. The Cathedral's towers were in sight, but the roads were wetter than ever the closer she got to Gloucester. Her clothes could hardly get any soggier, but she had to take care so she didn't get stuck again.

When she finally reached the Cathedral the service had ended and most of the people had gone. Lizzie's family must have thought her master was too mean to let her come home. The inside of the Cathedral was full of lovely flowers. Lizzie felt ashamed of her wet clothes, but there was something she had to do. She walked to the far end of the Cathedral, to the Lady Chapel. The daffodils and primroses on the altar glowed in the sunlight streaming through the windows. To say thank you to Mary, she laid her bunch of flowers on the altar and knelt down to pray. For her own mother she still had the cake.

It wasn't far from the Cathedral to her father's house. Lizzie was so looking forward to seeing her family. And she didn't want to miss out on the food. Hastily she splashed through the puddles and the mud. Her clothes couldn't get any wetter.

Or so she thought.

She stepped in a puddle. A puddle much deeper than it looked because of a pit in the road. The water came right up to her middle, she lost her footing, the basket was flung from her grip – and she tumbled full length into the water.

A man rushed to help her out. Dripping with muddy water, Lizzie remembered the simnel cake. Tears were spilling down her face as she retrieved the basket. The cake was ruined. It was ruined and now she wouldn't get her mother's blessing!

Everyone was there at her father's house: her brothers, sisters, nieces, nephews, aunties, uncles, grannies, all crammed into one room and tucking into the feast. When they saw Lizzie, soaked to the skin from head to toe, they all burst out laughing. Till her father saw she was crying and hushed them. Her mother whisked her upstairs to get her out of the wet clothes. But still Lizzie wept.

'What is it, child?' said her mother.

Lizzie showed her the cake. 'It's ruined, Mama. Now I can't have your blessing and my lady won't get half the blessing for giving me the ingredients.'

Her mother threw her arms around Lizzie and stroked her head. 'It's lovely that you made me a cake, but the best gift for me is just to see you again. I bless you with all my heart and may God bless you, too!'

5

THE MERMAID'S CURSE

The Wye is good for salmon in the spring. You can catch thirty-pounders or bigger as they run upriver. Many years ago, early in the morning before the river got busy with trows carrying goods down to Bristol, two boy-chaps from Brockweir went salmon fishing. They stretched a seine net between the two punts and each moored his punt by thrusting his pole through the prow hole. The net had wooden floats along the top and lead weights along the bottom to hold it vertical so the salmon coming upstream would swim into it.

Dick Hulin was hoping they'd catch lots of them. There'd be one for his mam, one for Isaac's, and the rest they'd sell to the river traders.

But before any salmon came, something else got caught in their net. Dick saw the silvery flick of a fish tail break the surface. It was too big for any salmon – even a whopper. There was a great splashing as the creature struggled to get free of the mesh. Dick had a funny feeling. No fish could be so big, could it? Whatever it was, he'd no wish to let it go.

He waved to Isaac. 'Tush now, butty!'

Dick pulled up the pole to release his punt from its mooring. He grabbed the oar and started paddling across to Isaac's boat to close the mouth of the net. As Isaac hauled in the net from his side, the struggling creature was trapped in a smaller and smaller space.

Suddenly the splashing stopped. The blighter must have got free! Couldn't have that! Dick heaved his oar with all his might. *Wap!* – the creature's tail was caught between the sides of the two punts. A shriek of pain.

The front half of the creature burst up from the water. It was the top half of a woman! A pretty one too, though her skin looked a bit scaly slimy and her hair was as white as Dick's granny's.

'Let me go!' she cried.

But Dick didn't want to let her go. A mermaid! People would pay good money just to come and see her. He pulled his end of the net loose and tried to throw it over her. The mermaid was too quick. With a flap of her tail she jerked up from between the boats, somersaulted through the air – a shimmering shimmy of woman and fish – and sliced back into the water.

From a safe distance her top half reared up again. She pointed a finger at Dick. 'If you had let me go,' she hissed, 'I'd have granted you a wish. Instead, the curse of the river be upon you! Very few of your descendants will die in their beds!'

Then she was gone. Feeling a bit shaken, Dick and Isaac gave up on the salmon and poled their punts back to the riverbank.

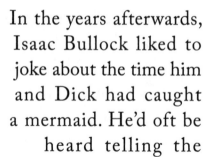

In the years afterwards, Isaac Bullock liked to joke about the time him and Dick had caught a mermaid. He'd oft be heard telling the story in one of Brockweir's seven alehouses. Dick didn't find it so amusing. Work on the river, whether on the trows or fishing, was dangerous. The tide could come in quick and high. They say that, back in the day when Brockweir was a busy port, the Wye took a man's life every month. When the one who drowned was a son or grandson or great-grandson of Dick Hulin, the old folks would say, 'That be the mermaid's curse as took 'im.'

Not so many years ago, a descendant of Dick's – let's call him Harry – was fast asleep upstairs in his cottage near what remains of

Brockweir's quay. He'd had a late night at the pub and it'd been raining when he staggered home to his warm bed. He slept and snored as the rain kept falling and the river began to rise. So high the water rose that it topped the riverbank, flooded the first gardens, and seeped under the door of Harry's house.

Then the tide came in from the Bristol Channel, pushing the water back upriver. Higher and higher the flood rose around Harry's house, and inside the house too – till the kitchen, living room and dining room were filled with water. In the darkness, as Harry snored in his bed, the water rippled along the landing and spilled up between the floorboards.

It was the knocking on his window that woke him. Some lads in a boat come to rescue him. In the gloom of early morning Harry could hear a sloshing noise all around him. He lowered one foot from the bed. Chill water! He snatched his foot back up.

'Hurry up, Harry!' called the lads. 'Get out while you can!'

Harry was afraid. He knew all about the mermaid's curse. His uncle was one of those taken by the river.

'I oultn't get out o' this bed!' he shouted to the lads at the window.

'You best come! The water still be rising!'

'No, I shall bide yur in my bed.'

So the lads had to think fast. While one gripped the window frame to stop the current carrying the boat away, the other two climbed into Harry's room. They sloshed shin deep through the water and dragged the mattress from the bed, Harry clinging on top of it, and heaved it through the window into the boat.

In the grey early light they rowed the boat to the grassy slope rising up to Brockweir House. Only then would Harry get off the mattress. He clambered over the gunwale to safety.

'I knew as I'd be all roight as long as I stayed in my bed, acoz of what that mermaid zed to awld Dick: "Very few of your descendants will die in their beds".'

6

CROCKET'S HOLE

It was May Day and the young folk had trooped up May Hill to be there for sunrise. The air was nippy. The sky was dark with cloud. Fiddle and flute were already playing. Mary Mayo was itching to start dancing. She and the other girls were waiting in a loose circle. The lads were pretending not to watch them.

Suddenly the music stopped. Everyone caught their breath and looked to the east. You could see right across to the Cotswold Edge, but there was no glimmer of sun through the grey cloud.

Maybe the flute player could see what others couldn't. He let out a shout and sprang into a lively tune. The fiddler joined in, his hand moving quick as the Devil. The girls began to dance. Soon their faces were pink and they'd cast off their woollen mantles. In the second tune, the lads danced too, those of them brave enough. Around and around – in and out – turn about – and snatch a quick kiss.

The dances were done, dawn had dawned, and still no sun. The girls sat down with lemonade and buns, while the young men organised the games: wrestling, running races, and a game of football that dragged on for hours … until at last the lads had to get ready for the battle.

The Winter King, crowned with holly, was dressed in thick woolly layers. His minions wielded bare branches, urged on by the dads striking the rough music of tongs and cleavers. The Summer King strode up in his yellow shirt and headdress of gaudy ribbons. His men carried leafy green branches, and the fiddle and flute were playing on his side. They advanced, two tribes, across the green grass. They hollered and yowled. They charged into the fray, Summer against Winter, the same battle every year.

What would happen, Mary wondered, if Winter should win? She didn't like the fighting, even if it was only pretend. What if some poor boy got hurt? She lay down on the grass and closed her eyes to the flat grey sky. The ground was solid against her back. She felt as though she was part of the hill. Only, the hill wasn't completely solid. Mary had been inside it. There was a hole in the ground, known as Crocket's Hole, hidden among the willows a little way down in the woods. She'd never dared descend more than a few rocky steps into the darkness.

Not like her old gaffers. Gramp Thomas and Gramp John had been best butties since they were boys. With a handful of stolen candles, they'd gone down into the tunnel. All sunlight lost behind them. Only the flickering gloom, grimy earth, cold slippery rocks, and the smell of rot. Sometimes the ceiling came so low they had to crawl on their bellies. Only *boys* would be so crazy as to keep going!

The reason? Treasure! It was supposed to lie halfway between Crocket's Hole and the tunnel's far end at Great Cugley. The boys were down to their last candle. Surely it couldn't be much further! They were starting to feel afraid …

Thomas and John both knew about Mr Witcomb, who'd come down here years before they were born. He'd had too much cider and boasted he could find the treasure. That's why people knew where to look when he disappeared …

Mr Witcomb was inspired by a story about a man who'd come to explore the tunnel back in the 1660s. He was a disbanded soldier. People called him 'Fairfax'. Who knows whether that was his real name or because he'd fought under Fairfax in the Civil War? He'd come all the way from London. He was convinced there was treasure down Crocket's Hole.

Now Crocket was a man who'd lived hereabouts a century yet earlier. That was when Protestants and Catholics hated each other because everyone thought their side was right and the other side was wrong. Queen Mary was Catholic. When she was queen, it was the Protestants' turn to get persecuted. Crocket was Protestant. So was his friend Horne. When the authorities were after them, they hid in the tunnel. It must have been in better shape back then. From the opening near Great Cugley, they'd collect food from Horne's wife. From Crocket's Hole they'd come out to stretch their legs on May Hill and read their copy of Tyndale's Bible.

Mrs Horne was expecting a baby. When the child was born, she gave a party to celebrate his baptism. Just a few friends and relatives, and the midwife. Unfortunately, the midwife was a busybody. She noticed that Mrs Horne had requested a cut of mutton that never got used at the party. The midwife guessed whom the meat was meant for, and went and told the Constable. The Constable came to the house after dark. He could hear a man's voice within. When he knocked on the door, there was a sudden noise of commotion. The Constable was too quick. He caught Horne trying to hide in a copper washtub, his head still poking from the top.

Poor Horne was tried for believing in the wrong religion, found guilty, and burnt at the stake in Newent. Mrs Horne quickly changed religion to save her life and prevent her children becoming orphans. But what about Crocket? The rumour was that Horne and he had stored a stash of coins in the tunnel so they and Horne's family could escape from England and start a new life in Holland, where it was fine to be Protestant. If Crocket had got away, had he taken the money with him?

Maybe Fairfax had found out that Crocket had left in such a rush that he'd left it all behind in the tunnel. Fairfax ventured some way down Crocket's Hole but he failed to find the treasure. Mr Witcomb never found it either. He was long dead when his body was discovered. Must have fallen asleep and died of cold.

It *was* really cold down here. By the light of their last candle Thomas and John came upon a stream rushing across their path. Beyond it something glinted in the candlelight. A rusty-looking metal box. It was almost in reach! Thomas stepped into the water. My, it was cold! Holding the candle in one hand, he stretched out the other to the box. Could almost touch it. How heavy would it be? He'd need two hands—

The slippery bed of the stream gave way under his shoe. Down he splashed. The candle flew from his hand – the little yellow flame arcing through the air – *fssst!* – into the water—

Darkness. Absolute blackness. Black as the grave. Thomas scrabbled out of the stream, hands blindly flailing, caught hold of someone.

'Be that thee, John?'

'Who else would it be, butty?'

They clung to each other in the darkness.

'We have to get out of this, John.'

'What about the treasure?'

'That stream do run fast and it be nation cold.'

In the darkness it was all they could do to work out which way was back. It was hard going. They kept bumping their heads on the tunnel walls. It was like being a mole, except they didn't have whiskers like a mole to help them find the way. It was uphill, too. At least the effort of climbing upwards helped to warm them. Crawling, crawling, along the smelly, slimy tunnel. The darkness so total you couldn't see your hand in front of your face. Thomas began to wonder if this was what it was like to be dead.

When at last they saw a pinprick of light they thought they were imagining it. But there it was, getting gradually bigger as they crawled towards it.

'That do be the way out!' croaked John.

Upward, onwards, they crawled and stumbled and staggered. The light at the end of the tunnel got bigger and brighter – till at last they could see the green of the ferns fringing the opening ...

The two gaffers had told Mary about that moment many times, as if it was the greatest thing ever, like they'd come back from the dead ... Here on the top of May Hill, where the May Day armies of Winter and Summer were still clashing and yelling, Mary opened her eyes – just as a shard of sunlight pierced the clouds. She held her breath and watched as the clouds wallowed and shifted like great ships in the sky. Then the sun came sailing out – the noontime sun, high and hot and bright.

A great cheer went up from the forces of Summer. Winter's men all dropped to the ground. The Summer King ripped the woollen wrappings from his opponent – till nothing was left of the Winter King save a skinny man whose chest gleamed white in the sun. All the girls and women, including Mary, lifted their hawthorn branches, thick with green foliage and white may blossom, to fête the Summer King who won the battle every year.

Then everyone joined in the Song of Joy, whose chorus goes:

The hedges and trees they are so green,
Where girls and boys do wander and roam.
A bunch of May we bring you, see!
We have brought the summer home!

They would carry on singing that all the way down to Newent, but first the elders of the parishes had to gather, here on May Hill, to decide which portions of common land should be allocated to which families for the coming year. It was a bit boring, but after all the excitement of the dancing, games, and battle, Mary enjoyed the peacefulness of this moment. There sat Gramp Thomas and Gramp John in a circle with the other old men, calmly deciding how to use the commons in a way that was fair for everyone. The day had got so sunny hot they had to keep on their hats in case their bald heads got burnt!

7

THE LAND
OF DREAMS

It was midnight, 11 May, the festival of
Lemuria, when back in Rome the head of
every household would rise from his bed to
placate the ghosts of those who'd died too
soon. Paulus was far away from Rome, here
in soggy Britain, in his farmhouse beside
Ermin Way, the road his brother Romans
had built straight as an arrow's flight
between Silchester and Cirencester. He was
neither father nor husband, he shared his
home only with his servants, yet at midnight
he got up and walked barefoot clockwise
round the house, as his father would do this

night. He snapped his fingers and threw a handful of black beans over his shoulder, taking care not to look back lest he see any ghosts behind him. Nine times he did this. Then he washed his hands and before the door he struck a bronze pot with a stick and called out, 'Ghosts of this house, begone!' Nine times he spoke the words. Then he took a deep breath and turned around.

Before him he saw only the grey gloom of the farmyard and, past the gate, the deeper shadows of the road and the trees. Any ghosts had vanished. Made bold by the ceremony and the moonlight now finding its way through the clouds, he walked a little way along the road. On the fresh night air came the smells of horse dung on the road and garlic from the woods between the fields. Soon the moonlight dimmed again behind the clouds. Paulus sat down upon a milestone. He began to feel afraid. There could be wild beasts in the darkness, a few last wolves or bears. There could be wild men too. Not all the British welcomed the

Romans who'd brought civilisation to their land. And what ghosts and spirits would haunt these woods and meadows and marshes, so remote from his home in Italy? What strange dreams would they inspire in the native people? Or in Paulus too when he tossed and turned in bed?

As he was thinking this, a pattern in the darkness resolved into a figure. Hooded she seemed, and gaunt and thin, though it was hard to be sure of anything in this gloom. Only that she beckoned to him. It seemed a kind of answer to his questions. He knew he must follow her! Across a field they tramped. A low hill loomed ahead. When the figure reached the trees on the rising ground, she stopped and turned. Moonlight gleamed on bony angles of her face.

Her voice was like a cackling wind: 'Do you seek the lands of shadow?'

'I do!' cried Paulus.

A black void opened in the hillside. His hooded guide led the way into what seemed like a chasm through mountains.

Downwards into the darkness they trudged. The Roman's heart quailed with fear, but it was too late to turn back.

They came to a place where the grey path parted three ways. The guide flung out her arm. 'Which way shall you go? To death, dream, or madness?'

Paulus chose the middle path; this night of Lemuria, his heart's desire was to understand the mystery of dreams. Silvery light glittered through the branches arching overhead. In a valley between mountains a sea of mist floated above a sluggish river. Nodding on the breeze were pale and purple flowers whose scents flooded his mind. Waterfalls plunged from crags so high that the water broke into soundless spray in mid-air. Fern leaves caressed his limbs. Moonish light sparkled on wet reeds ...

Suddenly before them stood a pillared palace of glittering white marble.

Through courtyard and corridor he came; his hooded guide had vanished. A curtain was drawn – and there, from a bronze throne, the Queen of Night stared down at him. Long-limbed and lovely in a star-spangled gown. Hair like a swirling black waterfall. The jewel of her circlet shining from her brow like Venus in the sky. In her hand a golden cup. Pale-faced owls and black-webbed bats swooped above her head. Vague ghostly forms drifted near her feet.

Paulus gazed open-mouthed. Never had he seen anyone so beautiful, not even in Rome! He had no words to voice his wonder. Her eyes ignited like windows of fire, beaming bright upon him like the light of sun and moon. He knew that all his thoughts were known. His mind was caught up in hers, and through her he saw what his own eyes could not – that from this palace he could reach where the dreams of men and women are born. His heart said YES! He must go. He must see.

With a flap of black wings, a creaking croak, a raven swept before the throne of Night. Like wind through the air, Paulus flew in the raven's wake. Through scenes

of scaly dragons and bristling beasts and shuddering, slimy ooze. Over sunny, sandy shores and washing white waves and bright leaping sparkles of schools of flying fish. The way spiralled in and in, like a serpent's coils, tighter and quicker came these images of Night's kingdom – till the raven spread her wings wide and they roofed the world.

In this black cave the silent dark pulsed with heartbeat and breath. Now Paulus was on his own. But he could feel *them* like a tingling all around him. He knew *them* in the million smells mingling in the air. He took a deep breath and opened his eyes and heart. From the black of the cave bloomed all the colours of the world. There he saw *them* – the dreams! In the form of men and women, girls and boys, they cried out, they wept, they crept and danced and laughed. They stared around wide-eyed in search of who knows what.

There was one who looked familiar, a young man. When this dream-man turned around, Paulus looked into the face of his own younger self. He was carried backwards down the path of life's arrow, to times before he ever worried about money and land, before he joined the army and came abroad, before he lost his first love ... There comes a moment when he's five years old and playing in the sun on a rocky beach. Strands of seaweed float in the rock pools, where sea anemones waft their pink tentacles and a crab skates along in a borrowed shell. Waves shush upon the shore, a seagull sings, and somewhere his mummy is near, and there's only happiness and love, and every dream he has could yet come true ...

Mist roils in from the sea. Clouds shutter the sun. Now darkness everywhere. He's tossed by unseen powers, through storm and sleet and the clash of ice and stone. He's lost and blind. Everything churning, moving. Have the dreamways brought him in the end to madness or death? There's a roaring of noise. There's thunder and gale. He shoots upwards like a stone from a catapult. From darkness he breaks into light and space, where a heavenly song swells and soars. And he is part of it. His heart is bursting like a bubble. The light too bright to look upon … Too much, too beautiful, for a mortal man …

Downwards he sped like a shooting star. His flames fizzed away as he dropped back into the silent black cave of dreams. For a few heartbeats he lingered there. Then he opened his eyes again. He was sitting on the milestone by Ermin Way. Five miles to Cirencester. A thousand miles to Rome. The birds were singing. The light of dawn glimmered between the trees. The shadows of the night were slinking away like ghosts into the depths of the woods. Bluebells and garlic peeped from the verge like a smile.

A stoat stopped and stared, beady-eyed, quicker-witted at this hour than the man. 'Be welcome,' it seemed to say. 'You have nothing to fear if you intend us no harm.' Then it raced across the Roman road and was gone.

8

THE IMMORTAL CAT OF CHIPPING SODBURY

'Third time's the charm,' muttered Thomas Norton. 'No one will disturb me here. I will live for ever!'

'Here' was Chipping Sodbury, a bustling market town in the 1460s. It wasn't Bristol, where everyone knew who Thomas was and what he did. Thomas was an alchemist. Not a chemist, giving out medicines, but a seeker for the magical elixir of life! Drink that and you would live for ever! Twice already had Thomas made it, after long study and careful work, and twice in Bristol had it been stolen from him! Well, not this time. In Chipping Sodbury, in these cramped rented rooms, no one knew his business. Thomas was sure he was safe.

The first theft he might have expected; servants could never be trusted. But the wife of his patron? Joan Canynges had always been hanging around Thomas's Redcliffe home when she should have been adorning her own, finer house, with its tall tower and bay windows overlooking the Avon. The foolish woman had seen her beauty begin to fade and hoped she could persuade him to share his secrets so she could stop time. He'd turned her away, but, instead of going back to her embroidery, she had taken matters into her own hands. She stole his elixir! But she didn't drink it. Her husband, the great Bristol merchant William Canynges, was building St Mary Redcliffe; she worried he'd spend all his money on that and leave her living for ever but with no money. So she waited, nagging William to stop. When sickness took her, and she went to drink her bottle of elixir, she found the liquid had long dried out …

Thomas felt it best to leave town in case he was blamed for her death.

'Mreow!'

Thomas looked down and frowned. The landlady's pesky ginger cat again, snaking round his legs as if the workings of alchemy would produce a special treat for the plump beast. He didn't want the animal anywhere near his delicate glass vessels and expensive potions.

'Shoo!' he said.

'Come away, Tom Tildrum!' cried his landlady. 'Don't trouble the gentleman.'

She scooped up the cat, babbling apologies as she bustled away. Another silly woman!

Thomas turned back to his work, carefully measuring out this liquid, grinding that stone into powder, blending, heating, bubbling. He worked all night. As the first grey fingers of dawn spread across the sky, three clear drops of liquid fell from his alembic into the waiting saucer.

Thomas gave a satisfied sigh. It was done. Immortality awaited. But right now he was tired. Setting the saucer on a shelf, he collapsed upon his bed and fell into a deep sleep.

He awoke to an almighty crash.

Disaster! All his vessels lay smashed on the floor ... And the saucer? On the floor. Empty. Disappearing around the door was a ginger tail ... With a groan Thomas buried his head in his hands.

'Foiled once more!' he muttered. 'I must seek a place where there are no servants, no women, and no cats!'

Tom Tildrum shot down the stairs to get away from the horrible smashing glass. Once out in the yard, he stopped and, with the concentration that only a cat has, began to wash his face. He could still taste that strange water from the saucer. It seemed to fizz in his mouth.

He felt amazing. He felt like he could catch a hundred mice. Mice? No! Rabbits? No! He felt like he could catch a hare! He wanted to go and yowl out his good health to all. So, being a cat, he did. He leapt upon the wall behind the house, pranced up and down, and sang.

He didn't even see the stone that hit him.

All he knew was the sharp pain in his head – and that he was flying through the air.

With a spin of his tail, he twisted mid-air and landed on his feet. He shook himself and stalked away. Then he saw the stone. He stopped and stared. Was that what had hit him? It was huge! He gave it a cautious sniff then jumped back, tail puffing out. It was covered in blood!

Tom licked a paw and washed his face. There was blood on his paw, but he still felt amazing! Then he realised what had happened. A blow like that should have killed him. But all that meant was that one of his nine lives was gone. No matter. He had eight more.

Time passed. Thomas Norton packed up and left Chipping Sodbury, heading for London and royal favour. Tom's mistress took in other lodgers to her house on the corner of Wickwar Road and the High Street. Tom lost a few more lives. Once he ran in front of a cart. Another time he ate something bad. He was bitten by a dog. Eight lives were lost. But he still felt wonderful, full of vim and spit and fight, even though he was nearly fifteen years old.

Then came the day when he was prowling around the market, waiting for morsels from the butchers' stalls to fall into his mouth – when a stall fell on him! His ninth life gone!

What a silly way to die!

He lay under the collapsed stall, hearing the shouts of men as if from a long, long way away. It all grew quieter … and then, there was light! Was this kitty heaven?

He blinked. No. It was the marketplace and they'd lifted the stall off him. He wasn't dead. He was fine! Up he bounced and shot away before anyone could blame him. When he got home, though, he licked a paw in puzzlement. How strange! His mother had told him that nine lives were all you got. But now he was on his tenth.

The years ticked by. No matter what life threw at him, Tom lived on. When his mistress died, he thought it best to move on. Down the road he sauntered, to Horse Street, and inveigled himself into the household of a weaver. He lived there for many years under the name 'Gib'. When he judged it time, he moved on once more. So it went on, a new home every few years, decade after decade, century after century ...

He was drawn to apothecaries. In his memory lingered the taste of that strange fizzy water all those years ago. He'd like another taste of that.

The tale was passed down, from apothecary to apothecary, that a ginger cat was always to be found about the place. You had to watch him, because he was always sticking his face in unsuitable potions.

When young Edward Jenner arrived on his apprenticeship in 1763, he saw a ginger tom prowling behind his lodgings on Horse Street. Jenner loved animals. He would fuss the cat, now known as Tim Toldrum, and feed him treats.

But one day a terrible thing happened. Edward was working in the still room for his master, Dr Daniel Ludlow, when Tim jumped on to the counter where some rat poison was set out in a dish.

'No!' cried Edward, and tried to shoo the cat away.

It was too late. Tim fell down by the dish.

Edward didn't know what else to do except run to fetch his master. Dr Ludlow was with a patient. By the time they arrived back the cat was gone.

'Probably tidied away by a servant, poor beast,' sighed Dr Ludlow. 'Ah well, Edward, no matter. His son'll come along soon to take his place. It always happens.'

Edward was devastated. He mourned poor Tim.

Then, one day, he saw Tim once more. He was certain it wasn't Tim's son. This cat had the same notch in his ear. But Edward had seen Tim die. He told the servants about it. Soon a rumour was running round Chipping Sodbury that the ginger tom was a ghost! Edward wasn't sure about that, but before long he left the town, on his way to becoming a doctor and the man who discovered the vaccine for smallpox.

Old Tom – now Tim – knew nothing of this. By the time Edward Jenner left he was living on the other side of town with an old widow. He kept on moving. For all I know, he's moving on still. Not so long ago, there was a chemist's in the same place on the corner of Wickwar Road where Tom's first mistress had lived, so back he went, hoping he might get another taste of that fizzy potion. The chemist's is on the other side of the High Street now. Maybe you'll see Tom there!

9

WHITSUN REVELS IN ST BRIAVELS

It was a time of war in England. Stephen was the king, but his cousin Matilda thought she should be queen instead. The lords of the west were on Matilda's side. Among them was Miles, Earl of Hereford, who'd welcomed Matilda when she arrived in Bristol from France. She had rewarded him by making him lord of St Briavels Castle and the Forest of Dean. Miles fought hard in Matilda's cause and won many battles.

But war is a terrible time for the common people. Food was scarce and the families of St Briavels often went hungry. More than ever, they depended on their time-honoured rights on the commons, such as the right to collect firewood in the Hudnalls woods just outside the village. They needed the firewood to cook their food and warm their homes.

For Miles, all that mattered was the war. Resources like wood were needed for his soldiers. It was not a time to be worrying about the needs of poor folk. He banned the people from gathering wood in Hudnalls.

Someone who did worry about the ordinary people of St Briavels was Miles's wife, Sybil, Countess of Hereford. From the windows of the castle she watched them go about their business. She knew how hard their lives were. She was a godly lady, who prayed every day in the chapel.

She pleaded with her husband: 'Will you not let the people collect wood in Hudnalls? While the men toil in your fields and struggle to put food on their own tables, the women have to walk many miles into the Forest to get firewood – even old widows who hardly have the strength to walk.'

'We're fighting a war!' declared Miles. 'We must apply everything in our power to the cause of victory. To worry about old widows is a luxury we cannot afford.'

'But *we* in this castle yet have our luxuries. We have all the food, firewood and fine clothes we need.'

'*We* are not the common folk, Sybil. You know that. You would not forgo the privileges of your rank.'

There was a long silence, then Sybil quietly said, 'I would forgo everything I have if it would soften your heart towards the people.'

Miles stared at her. 'What do you mean?'

In Sybil's mind was a story of a lady in Coventry many years before. 'I mean that in this cause I would take off my fine clothes and ride through the streets in nature's garb.'

'You would not dare!' cried the Earl.

'Out of pity for the people, I would.'

Miles proudly folded his arms. 'Let you ride unclothed through the village streets this Whit Sunday and I will grant each household the right to gather in Hudnalls as much wood as they wish in return for a payment of one penny per year. But I know you shall never do such a thing.'

Some would say that to go without clothes would be shameful before God, but Sybil knew that Adam and Eve had been naked in the Garden of Eden. Just as God was the maker of all people, so God wouldn't want them to suffer. God had sent Jesus to the poor and needy; and Whit Sunday celebrated how God sent the Holy Ghost to fill people's hearts with joy.

On Whit Sunday morning, Sybil could hear music and laughter in the streets outside the castle. The people were doing their best to keep the Whitsun custom of merrymaking in spite of their hardships.

Sybil's mind was made up. The preparations had been made. In the stable, beside her white horse Alfgar, she took off her clothes and let down her long hair. Trembling, she climbed the mounting block and sat astride Alfgar's back. She touched his sides with her bare heels to make him go. Out in the castle yard, the sun was hot on her white skin that had never seen the sun. Her heart was pounding, but the power of the horse beneath her and the sun above her gave her courage.

From the gatehouse she rode out to the market square where people were dancing to the music of pipe and drum. At once the music stopped. All dancing and laughter came to a halt. The only sounds were the

wind in the trees and the clip-clop of Alfgar's hooves.

Sybil had feared that people might laugh and stare. But as she rode slowly along the High Street every man, woman and child respectfully bowed their head. The only one who didn't was a baby in his mother's arms, who beamed a bright smile as Sybil passed.

Back down Pystol Lane she rode. One by one the people fell in to follow her, eyes lowered, a silent procession. Past the alehouse they went, and along Church Street, the castle towering on their left. At the church, Sybil slid down from Alfgar's back. From the hot sunshine she stepped into the coolness of the church. Sunlight glowed through the stained-glass window from which Mother Mary and Baby Jesus smiled down.

Sybil put on the clothes her servant had earlier brought to the church – a chemise and cotte, both pure white, like the light of the Holy Ghost shining in her heart. While she knelt in prayer before the altar, the people filed into the church. There was a clinking as pennies dropped into a box held by the verger at the door. The priest came to take the Whit Sunday service. Everyone stood and knelt and said 'Amen' when they should.

Then the verger and another man appeared on the rood loft, a wooden platform high above the congregation. The verger called out, 'With the compliments of Countess Sybil!' They began to throw down pieces of bread and cheese. Suddenly there was mayhem and laughter as everyone leapt about to catch them.

Meanwhile, from the battlements of his castle, Miles had seen what his wife had done. He was a hard man, a warrior, but also a man of his word. When the verger brought him the pennies paid by the people of St Briavels, he granted them – as he'd promised – the right to collect firewood in Hudnalls as their fathers and mothers had always done.

That right has continued ever since. So too has the dole of bread and cheese thrown to the parishioners on Whit Sunday. These days, to avoid a mess in the church, the pieces of bread and cheese are thrown from the churchyard wall. St Briavels miners often kept them all year as a charm against accident. Others put them under their pillow in hope of dreams of what the future might bring.

In 1992, there were plans to change the parish boundary. The remaining Hudnalls woods would be in a different parish and the people of St Briavels would no longer be allowed to collect firewood there. They had to fight to protect the ancient right won for them more than eight hundred years ago by the brave Countess of Hereford.

10

PUCK OF PAGANHILL

All was in readiness on the Green in Paganhill that Whitsuntide. The maypole was up, as tall as a church spire! It was decked with flowers and ribbons, and a weathercock turned this way and that at the top. The Crown had opened its doors, the band were tuning up, and all the villagers were gathering.

Valentine Taylor was nervous. He'd come all the way from Bristol, invited by the family who lived in the fine house by the Green. He wasn't used to village life. He was a merchant's son, more used to fine parties in the tall houses of Queen Square.

These farmers in their smocks, laughing and talking loudly in broad Gloucestershire, made him feel foolish.

Then something bright caught Valentine's eye. Down the hill towards the Green came a bevy of young women, all dressed in white and pink and blue and as decked with ribbons as the maypole. One of them shone above all the others. She was so pretty he couldn't take his eyes off her. As the girls passed him she turned and smiled! Cupid struck young Valentine's heart with an arrow. Love swelled in his heart.

He turned to his host and cried, 'Who is that fair Flora?'

'Some shepherdess, no doubt.'

Valentine watched eagerly as the girl danced with her sister shepherdesses around the maypole. How he wished he could speak to her! As the fiddle struck up the next tune, other people on the Green were drawn into the circle dance.

Shyly he approached the maypole. Someone seized his hand. Suddenly he was dancing! When he looked up, he saw it was his shepherdess who'd taken his hand.

'My Flora!' he cried.

The girl laughed. 'My name, sir, be Kate, not Flora!'

All that day they danced and by the end of it they were in love. Valentine didn't want to say goodbye – so he asked Kate to marry him.

'For 'tis you I love, Kate. I will love none other.'

Blushing, Kate ducked her head and said that she loved him too. Straight up the hill she took him to her father's house near Puckshole Mill. If Valentine had thought that country folk lived well, when he stepped inside the single room that Kate, her father, and her brothers and sisters shared, he saw they did not. It didn't matter. Kate stood like a beacon of light and beauty as he asked her father's permission to marry her.

'But sir,' said her father, 'we'm poor folk. Kate ain't got no dowry.'

Valentine waved his hand in dismissal. 'I have money aplenty – at least my father does.'

His father was furious. He refused to let them marry. Valentine was determined. His father shouted and swore, but Valentine shook his head.

'We will be married, whether you like it or not.'

'Marry your penniless peasant girl, then,' raged his father. 'But you'll have no money from me. If you want her, you must provide for her yourself.'

It was a sad Valentine who made his way back to Puckshole. He could barely look Kate in the face when he told her what his father had said.

'Kate, I'm no catch now. I have nothing but the clothes on my back.'

She touched his cheek. 'Thee must go back to Bristol, my love. I can't bring ee down like this. A poor girl like me shouldn't be a-marrying a rich man like thee.' Tears rolled down her cheeks. 'Thy father be right. It goes against the natural way of things.'

Suddenly Valentine was angry. He grasped her hand. 'No! If you still want me, as poor as I now am, I swear I will work day and night to keep us. Nothing will be too hard if we're together.'

Kate's smile was like the sun coming out from behind a cloud. For Valentine there was no brighter thing in the world.

As they went into her father's house neither heard the rustling and whispering in the trees by the stream, or the cackle of laughter that followed.

Kate and Valentine were married, and Valentine came to live in her father's house at Puckshole. Every morning, he awoke before dawn to hear the millstream babbling behind the house. His father-in-law worked for a farmer up in the hamlet of Bread Street, and now Valentine worked for him too. It was the kind of work he could never have imagined when he lived in luxury in Bristol.

That June he mowed the hay and helped shear the sheep. It was hard work! In August and September came the harvest. That was harder work still! Meanwhile, Kate took the sheep to the meadows that sloped down below Whiteshill, and milked the farmer's cows. The farmer gave them little milk, but each night she placed outside the door a little saucer of cream.

'For the fairies,' she told Valentine.

He laughed. 'So there really is a Puck at Puckshole!' But he didn't really believe it.

Come winter the little cottage was cramped and cold. Valentine never complained. He was proud his labour brought money into the house and helped feed the family. At Christmas he gave Kate a brooch that had belonged to his mother, and she told him that, come Whitsun, or a little after, he'd be holding his first child in his arms.

'It'll be a bit cramped in this house,' she said, watching his face. 'But thee mustn't worry. We'll find room, and all will be well.'

Valentine smiled and kissed her …

But when he went down to the trees by the stream to gather firewood he began to cry. He whispered to the brook that he wished he could offer his child – and Kate – more than this poor life.

There was a rustle and a giggle in the undergrowth, a flash of red between the bare trees, but Valentine was already trudging back to the house.

In February, Valentine learnt to plough the fields ready for the new crops, and he took over Kate's job of helping with the lambing, saying, 'You must care for our own lamb now.' He was out every day in the freezing wind and snow. Late one evening, darkness long fallen, he was plodding wearily back down the big arable field in Bread Street with the oxen and plough. Suddenly, he saw a flash of red. He stopped dead. Right in front of him stood a little old man with a long white beard down to his knees and a knobbly stick in his hand. The man was no bigger than a six-year-old child and dressed in the brightest red suit Valentine had ever seen.

Valentine guessed who this must be.

'So you're Puck?' he breathed.

'Oh yes, 'tis I,' said the old man. 'And I know you, Valentine Taylor.' He poked at Valentine with his stick. 'We been a-watching you right from when you offered for young Kate who looks after us so kindly with her saucers of cream! We been not sure 'bout you, fancy Bristol fellow as ye be, as our folk be not so welcome in cities no more. But – you've done her right, worked hard and made yourself useful, so I've some advice for ye. Take that plough, drive it hard by the old stone wall to where the old beech tree stands, and ye shall see what ye shall see. Do it tonight! The chance shall not come again.'

Valentine blinked – and between the closing and opening of his eyes the little man was gone.

He hardly knew what to think. The fairies were real! And they were offering him – what?

Only one way to find out!

He turned the oxen around and led them back up the field, retracing the plough's path in the furrows, till he reached the old wall in question. Along the wall they went, the plough stuttering through the cold earth until, with a chink, something stopped it. The yoke yanked the oxen back and they let out a plaintive moo.

Valentine dropped to his knees and with his bare hands he scrabbled at the frozen earth. He felt something! A pot! As he lifted it up, there spilled out shiny gold coins!

He couldn't believe his eyes. Tightly clutching the pot, he hurried the oxen and plough home.

Imagine Kate's surprise when he showed her the ancient gold the next morning!

'Roman gold coins!' he cried. 'They've been there since long before the farm. It's down to you we have them, my love, because you put out that cream every night. It's a gift from the Puck of Paganhill so that you, me, and our little lamb can live well!'

11

THE COTSWOLD OLYMPICKS

Lucy Lillie would always remember the year she was the youngest dancer at Dover's Games up on the hill by Chipping Campden. She was only eleven, but she'd been dancing since she could walk, and she loved it. Besides, not that many girls were put forward. By 1636 there were some who said dancing was the Devil's work.

The Games were known as a 'Cotswold Olympicks'. Lucy was to be a dryad in the dance. She didn't know what that meant, but she knew they'd be dancing before old Dover himself. As the youngest girl, she was to present him with an oak leaf crown at the end. She was a little nervous about that. As she waited to start dancing she plucked at her heavy lace ruff and squinted up at the cloudless sky. If only it weren't so hot this Whitsuntide!

There was another thing worrying her. This year her brother James was in the wrestling. He was eighteen; it was his first time as well. The wrestling was on after her dance – but right on the other side of the Games. Lucy didn't want to miss it.

The other girls were all older than her and hadn't spoken to her all day. They were whispering about Prince Rupert, the King's nephew, who it was said might be coming, and how handsome he was supposed to be.

Lucy adjusted her beech leaf chaplet and stepped into position among the girls. The lute and viol started up. The dance began. She could see Mr Dover smiling and nodding in time to the music as they twirled.

When the music stopped she stood beaming for a moment. She hadn't missed a step and all the gentry were clapping. Two boys in green doublets came and placed the crown in her hands. Flanked by the boys, she crossed to the seated figure in his rich golden suit.

Up close his face was lined, and red from the heat, but he was still smiling.

Dipping into a curtsey, she said what she'd been told: 'Here is a timely offering from our Grove, an oak coronet to crown our Dover.'

Dover threw back his head and laughed. Lucy felt small and wasn't sure what to do with the crown. At last Dover swept off his feathered hat and bowed his grey head so she could crown him.

'Well danced, young Terpsichore!' He pressed a pouch into her hand. 'You should save that for your dowry, but perhaps a few pence on ribbons and Whitsun cakes won't go amiss.'

He and his entourage of gentry moved on. Lucy stood clutching the purse and wondering what he'd called her. Then she remembered her brother.

'Mama! It be nigh time for the wrestling! We have to go!'

'Not in that dress, Lucy. Let's get thee changed – or thee must spend thy prize on a new one.'

'Mama, come *on*!'

It took for ever to get off the heavy embroidered dress, but at last Lucy was back in her own blue dress and lace-trimmed apron and collar.

Without waiting for her mother, she plunged into the crowds. She knew her way around the Games. Up past Dover's wooden castle that had opened the fair with cannon shots. Along by the gaming tents. By the paddock, where they were grooming the horses for the next race. The hunting dogs were going mad, barking and barking as they waited to course the hares. Past the stalls she ran – the Whitsun cakes smelt so good! Past the turf maze. Till there at last was the wrestling arena, and James. He looked cross. She was sure she'd missed it.

'I'm sorry!' she cried. 'It took *for ever* to get changed.'

He caught her up in his arms.

''Tis all right, Lucy. Tain't 'appened yet. Now we best come away. They've sent for the guards …'

Someone was shouting loudly. Some strange-looking people were in the wrestling arena, dressed all in black save for their white collars. They looked very plain, like crows in a field of jays.

One of the men was shouting, 'These fairs are a profanation of the sacred feasts of the Lord. 'Tis against the law of God that ye gather today for this immoderate play! Wrestling! Dancing! Acrobatics! Such things are the Devil's work!'

Someone knocked against Lucy and she wriggled free of her brother's grip. Ignoring his shout, she darted through the press of people to get a better look. Why did people think dancing was the Devil's work?

While the man shouted, the men and women with him moved around the crowd, handing out pamphlets.

'Know ye that last year in Churchdown a miller, against his minister's admonitions, kept a Whitsun ale with revels, and that very night as they danced a fire started in his roof and burnt down the house – and all the folks within! Let that be your lesson! The retribution of the Lord is nigh!'

Lucy looked up. The once blue sky was now black with clouds. God must be coming!

Then men in Dover's livery with cudgels burst into the crowd, grabbed the protesters, and hauled them away.

'King Charles himself supports these Games,' one of Dover's men cried. 'Would you speak ill of the King?'

Lucy had heard enough. She turned to push through the crowd. At that moment one of the women flung her pamphlets into the air. They were caught in the quickening wind and scattered across the hill.

'Lucy! Thank heavens!'

There was her brother – and her mother. She leapt into her mother's arms and felt them close tight around her.

'They said God was going to smite us and now the sky be all black!'

As she spoke, a man shouted that the wrestling was to begin. No time to feel afraid, because James and his opponent were first up. The crowds formed a circle around the wrestlers and joined arms.

The first spots of rain fell. Soon it was coming down in sheets. People were shouting all over the hill, but Lucy hardly heard them. James and his opponent were locked together, kicking at each other's shins as each tried to force the other down to the muddy ground. Lucy held her breath, excited and afraid at the same time.

James won his first bout. Lucy cheered with the rest, all fear of God's wrath forgotten. James went on to win his next round. By now all the wrestlers were covered in mud. Lucy and her mother were soaked, but it didn't matter, because James was in the final!

She thought she'd burst with pride when he won and went up to Dover, just as she had, to get his prize money. The rain had stopped. The sky was blue again. Beside Dover was a tall, handsome young man with long dark hair who smiled and said a few words to James. James bowed low. Lucy's mouth dropped. Was it – Prince Rupert?

James came back, grinning and chinking the money in his purse.

'Whitsun cakes be on me!' he cried.

They hurried to the stall, still piled with cakes. All over the muddy ground were the Puritans' pamphlets, soggy and trampled.

'Cakes yent selling as they were' – the stallholder waved a pamphlet – 'acoz of these Puritans. Gentryfolk'll support the Games, but I reckons the country be about to explode. Who knows if we'll be here next year?'

Lucy wasn't listening. She bit into the cake and tasted the juicy, spicy currants. As she munched, the pamphlet blew away on the breeze.

12

A CANDLE IN
THE WINDOW

It was the days of the Civil War. England
was divided between the Royalists, who
fought for the King, and the Roundheads,
who fought for Parliament. For two long
years the war had raged and neither side
had won victory. Gloucestershire was
divided just as the kingdom was divided.
Much of the county was for the King,
but a Roundhead garrison commanded
by Colonel Massey held Gloucester. For
a whole month in the summer of 1643
the King had besieged the city. To trick
the Royalists that Gloucester had plenty

of food, when in truth the people were starving, Massey had a pig chased all over the city; its squealing everywhere made it sound like they still had dozens of pigs whereas in fact it was the only one left.

Parliament held a few other places in the county, including Chavenage House, near Tetbury, whose owner, Nathaniel Stephens, had raised a regiment of cavalry. Little more than a mile away over the fields, its towers clearly visible from Chavenage, stood the Royalist stronghold of Beverston Castle.

One of the serving maids at Chavenage was a girl called Rosie. She was seventeen. The housekeeper kept her busy most of the day, but late some evenings, when she had time free, Rosie liked to walk in the garden and woods behind the house. One evening in early spring of 1644 she took the wrong path in the gathering dark and walked further than usual from the house.

As she dithered how to get back, she heard something among the trees – a horse's whickering, quickly shushed by a man's voice. A man, a stranger, and she out here alone!

He stepped out of the shadows. Floppy hat, long hair, riding boots – a Royalist Cavalier – and in his hand his bared sword!

'It's Rosie, isn't it?' A strong northern voice of command.

When he came nearer she saw who he was.

'Master Oglethorpe?'

'It's *Colonel* Oglethorpe now.'

Rosie remembered Sutton Oglethorpe from when he'd come to stay at Chavenage before the war. He'd charmed her with his sparkling eyes, made her feel she was special among all the servants. Now he was on the King's side in the war. Commander of Beverston Castle, no less.

'What are you doing here, sir?' she blurted.

'Never you mind about that, Rosie. Perhaps I was hoping to meet you.'

Her heart melted then. She didn't care he was a Royalist. He sheathed his sword and talked to her sweetly. He looked so dashing in the moonlight with his curly moustache and long flowing hair. When he kissed her she thought her heart would burst.

Too soon he had to go. 'But it would be nice to see you again another night.' Rosie wanted that more than anything. 'The thing is,' he said, 'I'll need to know the coast is clear. I don't want to get caught by the Roundheads if they make a night raid against Beverston. But on nights when I know there's no danger of an attack I can come to meet you.'

So they agreed a plan. Evenings when Rosie knew there'd be no attack, she would light a candle in a porch window of Chavenage House that could be seen from Beverston Castle. Then Oglethorpe would know it was safe to come out across the fields.

Of course, he was very busy as commander of Beverston. There were many evenings when Rosie, having lit the candle in the porch, waited in the woods, hoping he would come, till she got too cold to wait any longer. But it was worth it for those special times when her handsome Cavalier came to her. Soon they began to meet in a hay barn where they had shelter from the rain and cold while they kissed and cuddled.

On the nights when Rosie knew that Master Stephens was planning an attack against Beverston, she would light no candle in the porch window and stay safely indoors.

It was a mystery to Stephens that whenever he attempted an evening raid on the farms and barns around Beverston Castle the Royalist soldiers would always be ready. As soon as the Roundhead troopers came too near, there'd be the crack and bang of gunpowder, musket balls would zing through the air, and they'd quickly have to ride away before any horses or men got hit.

Beverston Castle was a cause of concern to Stephens's superior, Colonel Massey in Gloucester. Its position meant the Royalists controlled the road between Bristol and Oxford and between Gloucester and the south. If Parliament could take Beverston, it might help turn the tide of the war.

Massey gathered a force of three hundred foot soldiers, eighty horsemen, and two cannons. Arriving at Chavenage, he talked with Stephens about strategy. Under cover of dusk, the Roundhead force manoeuvred along the lanes and through the fields and orchards. The castle and surrounding buildings were silent and still. Maybe too silent.

Massey positioned the cannons so they were aimed at the castle gate. A squad of fifty musketeers were ready with a petard – a bomb full of gunpowder – which they were to plant at the foot of the gate. If the gateway could be blasted open the Roundheads should be able to take the castle by force of numbers. At Massey's signal the cannons roared. The musketeers stumbled forwards through the gloom. The fuse of the petard was lit—

But the drawbridge had been raised! They couldn't get across the moat! Suddenly something was hurled down from the ramparts. Bang! Then more of them – grenades – exploding all around! The men carrying the petard – 'ONE, TWO, THREE!' – lobbed it across the moat. There was a terrific BANG that made the ground shake. But the petard had fallen short of the gate. Useless! More grenades came exploding down. Muskets fired from the battlements and loopholes. It was a shambles!

The trumpeter sounded the retreat and the attacking force withdrew. Quick march down the road to Wotton. Massey was furious. How had the Royalists known an attack was coming? He said to Stephens afterwards, 'Be on your guard! They must have spies.'

Soon after that, Massey and his troops had to move on to fight elsewhere. Stephens, meanwhile, was fretting about spies.

One evening, he took a tour of the house, checking doors and windows, making sure the guards were awake. As he stepped into the passage to the library, he saw someone inside the porch of the garden door. Soft-footed, he stepped back and watched. It was young Rosie. She was lighting a candle in the little

window in the porch. Why was she doing that? Quickly Stephens went to the guardroom to speak to the men on the evening watch.

After she'd lit the candle, Rosie waited in the scullery till enough time had passed. Then she slipped outside. In the barn, Sutton Oglethorpe was waiting, handsome as ever in the moonlight from the window.

'Ah, my sweet Rosie, I so wanted to see you!'

She sensed at once that something was wrong.

'Is anything the matter?' she asked.

'I'm afraid so, my poppet. I'm to be relieved of my command. Sir Baynham Throckmorton is on his way to take over. I don't know the reason why.'

Rosie's heart quailed. 'Does this mean you must go away?'

'I expect that it will. No doubt the King will find some other job for me in this war.'

She clung to him and wept. She believed that Sutton loved her; had hoped that, though she was only a serving girl, he might marry her.

Suddenly the door burst open. Light from a lantern lit up the barn as half a dozen men-at-arms rushed in. They had swords and pistols drawn. There was nothing Oglethorpe could do. Six armed guards against one man in his shirtsleeves. He surrendered without a fight.

A couple of days later Colonel Massey received word that Oglethorpe had been captured. Throckmorton had yet to arrive at Beverston, so the castle was without a commander. What's more, it seemed the 'spy' had been captured too. Massey sent orders for a unit of troops to march from Ross-on-Wye and then he rode back at speed to Gloucestershire.

Meanwhile, at Chavenage, Nathaniel Stephens had locked up Rosie in an empty pighouse. He'd guessed the purpose of the candle in the porch window. There was a clear line of sight from there to Beverston Castle.

Massey and the men from Ross arrived on the 23rd of May. Having heard the story, Massey knew what to do. Oglethorpe would surely have told his sergeants that a candle flame in the window was a signal there would be no attack. At dusk Massey lit a candle in that same window where Stephens had seen Rosie light one.

Under cover of darkness Massey led his men to Beverston. Faint sounds of talking and laughter could be heard in the castle. Nothing stirred in the outbuildings. The Roundhead troops took up their positions. Cannons were trained on the gatehouse.

Massey fired a pistol shot into the air. There was sudden commotion within the castle – voices shouting, footsteps stumbling.

Aha! thought Massey. At last we have you by surprise!

In a loud voice he called out, 'Hear this! Colonel Oglethorpe has been captured. You are surrounded by troops loyal to Parliament. You cannot escape. Surrender now and I give you my solemn word you will not be harmed and I shall let you proceed to whichever Royalist garrison you choose.'

With no commander, and taken by surprise, the soldiers in the castle surrendered without a fight. When they'd handed over their weapons, they were allowed to tramp away in their shirtsleeves to Malmesbury, a town held by the King.

As for Rosie, she was dismissed from the household of Nathaniel Stephens because she'd sent secret signals to the enemy. Chavenage had been her home since she was a child. She didn't know what to do. No one would tell her what had happened to Sutton Oglethorpe. She heard that the men from Beverston had gone to Malmesbury. Perhaps he'd gone with them. So she trudged along the lanes towards Malmesbury, begging crusts of bread, drinking water from village wells.

Sutton Oglethorpe did survive the Civil War. But because – with the King's defeat – he was on the losing side, he was stripped of his land and his house in Yorkshire. He lived long enough to see his fortunes improve when a new king returned to England in 1660. I'm sorry I can't tell you what became of Rosie. I doubt she ever found Oglethorpe. Maybe she had family somewhere. Maybe she was able to find refuge with them amidst this desperate time of war.

13

THE GREAT SEA SERPENT OF COOMBE HILL

Everyone around The Leigh knew the story of how, long ago, a dragon had terrorised nearby Deerhurst. Some had even seen the stone dragons in the church! But that was ancient history. Weren't such things – dragons, giants, monsters – just fairy tales?

That summer it rained and rained, and then it rained some more. At first, the villagers and farmers welcomed the rain, but as it continued to pour they began to get worried. They lived next to a mighty river, the Severn, and the land around them was already marshy and flooded easily. In winter the place was flooded most of the time. But in summer? Well, they knew what to do. They moved their cattle off the marshes and got out the sandbags.

None too soon! On the third night of rain the river burst its banks and spilled across the land. But this was no ordinary flood. The water kept on coming. Even people in Coombe Hill and by the Gloucester Road began to worry it would come into their homes. For several days the floodwaters rose. The river looked like a sea stretching as far as you could see. People kept to their houses and prayed.

At last the water began to recede. What a wreck the land was! Everywhere mud and uprooted trees. So much for the rich, marshy summer grazing for the cattle. Still, nothing to be done but put it to rights. The villagers and farmers rolled up their sleeves and set to work.

The marshes were quieter than usual. Usually you'd hear the singing of the birds, the drone of the insects, the lowing of the cattle, but now, silence. It stood to reason, everything was gone, but it felt eerie. The closer to the river you got, the eerier it felt. It was mostly silent there, but now and then there rose up a terrible screeching.

'Wading birds,' said the farmers to each other, with nervous nods.

People began to say there was something out there. Something could be seen moving between the ragged, mud-caked willows, they said.

Then livestock started to go missing. Farmer Bayliss's prize cow disappeared overnight. There were mutterings in The Leigh that people were thieving after the floods.

Then one of the workers in the marshes, an old man, went missing. The searchers found only a foot. They saw it had been chewed.

Something had come up the river in the floods. Something big. Something with long, sharp teeth. A dragon? Again? Really? But it wasn't.

Jim Gaskin and Tony Trapp saw it first. They rushed into the Swan at Coombe Hill, screaming, 'There's a sea monster! A great scaly sea serpent! What're we going to do?'

The villagers stopped going down there, they kept their livestock away, but word soon got out. People flocked from Gloucester and Tewkesbury to have a squinny at the monster. The serpent kept to itself in the marshes. People were disgruntled when they didn't see it, so the women of the village started knocking up little cloth serpents to sell, and the potter made mugs with serpent handles. Soon they were making a packet, but the monster was still rampaging in the marshes and the villagers were afraid it would never leave.

One of those visitors was Tom, a blacksmith from Cheltenham. He bought a cloth serpent for his baby sister and a mug for himself. He settled down in the Swan to test the mug with some of the landlord's best bitter. While he was there, someone told the story of the Deerhurst dragon.

Tom thought to himself, 'I could do that! I'll kill the serpent and be a hero!'

Only thing was, he said it out loud. The villagers leapt at the chance. Tom found he was a hero in the making. His fellow blacksmith at Coombe Hill gave him an axe, an old metal saucepan was slapped on his head, and a haunch of roast pork produced as a lure. Before he knew what he was about, he was packed off into the marshes.

His heart hammered. His head hurt. His feet squelched in the mud along a willow-lined path. He didn't dare run away. Men from Coombe Hill and Deerhurst Walton and The Leigh had seen him off. There was no way out. He was a strong man, but a sea serpent would be stronger … He imagined an awful scaly beast, full of savage teeth.

A terrible screeching filled the air.

He froze.

'What was that?' he whispered.

Quaking, he inched along until the path led out of the marsh to a reedy pool.

There, in the middle of the water, swam the serpent.

She was beautiful. Her scales glimmered blue and green and silver. Her neck was long and snaky. Her head, uplifted and cocked to look at him, was surprisingly dainty. He stood entranced as she glided through the reeds towards him. As she drew closer and opened those dainty jaws, he saw down a dark red throat that was getting bigger all the time …

With a shout of terror he flung the haunch of pork at her and fled.

She made disgusting noises as she fed.

Tom ran, but soon he heard the sound of her flippers dragging over the ground.

He was done for!

He felt a nudge in his back. With a shriek he spun around – to see her scooting back to the reeds, looking just as afraid. For a long, tense moment they stared at each other. Her eyes were big and full of longing. For a moment he was minded of his dog, Rags, when she wanted a snack.

'You want more pork?' he wondered.

He was sure that she nodded.

Back to the village he fled. There he gabbled out that he had a plan and he needed more pork.

As he approached the pool the second time, he saw her muzzle lift and sniff.

It was sobering to watch her jaws tear up the pork.

Next day, she was waiting on the land, drooling as she eyed the meat.

After a week, he could stroke her scales. They felt smooth and cool.

His plan had worked. He'd won her confidence. But now it came to it he couldn't bear to actually kill her.

Back he went to the village. 'She almost trusts me! This time I'll get her for sure!'

Instead of one haunch, he loaded up a whole barrow of pork. Carefully he wheeled it through the mud.

The serpent's head rose up at the smell. He wheeled it away from her along the muddy path to the river. A slithery splashing told him she was following.

The Severn when they reached it was sluggish and full. The serpent's head lifted and she screeched.

'That's it, my beauty!' cried Tom. He chucked up a pork haunch to encourage her.

Her head snapped up, catching the morsel and gulping it down.

The next one he threw towards the river.

She slithered down the steep slope through the willows – straight into the water. She caught the pork just before it splashed in. Then she seemed to realise what had happened and dove deep into the water. Tom laughed to see her delight at being back in the river.

Suddenly the serpent was back at the bank, eyes questioning.

'Time to go, my lovely,' he whispered.

Still the serpent stared.

He looked at the broad back at the base of her long neck and wondered. Then he shrugged. Ah well, he'd come this far! She seemed to know what he was about, and waited patiently as he clambered on.

She gave him the ride of his life! Along
the Severn they swam, riding the water
like the fastest sailing ship! Soaked and
shouting, he clung to her neck. Past him
flashed Gloucester, Minsterworth, the river
widening, the swell deepening, past Lydney,
and onwards to the Bristol Channel! It was
so exciting he wasn't scared she might dunk
or drop him.

As they approached the Channel, though,
he began to get alarmed.

'Stop!' he cried. 'I can't go out to sea! I'll
drown out there!'

Her head cocked to one side, and suddenly they were heading to the bank. The tide was high. He was able to scramble ashore. She bowed her head to him, and he to her. Dripping and shaking, he watched her glide back to the main channel and dive down.

He watched the waters, but she was gone.

He was cold and had a long, long walk back, but he didn't care. As for the villagers back in Coombe Hill, he might not have a head to show them, but they couldn't argue, could they? He *had* got rid of the serpent.

14

A MIDSUMMER NIGHT'S WATCH

Midsummer's Eve that year was going to be a strange one. John de Folewell rammed another branch into the wake-fire they were building. It would be his first time to stay awake beside it all night. It shouldn't have been him. It should have been his brother, William. But William was dead and John had to take his place. John had been working on his father's fields on the Lady of Minchinhampton's land for two years now. Ploughing, weeding, haymaking. He could do the job, but he so wished William was here. They'd never been apart, almost like twins. William had stood watch on this the shortest night for the first time last year. He'd been the same age John was now – fourteen.

John felt a hand on his shoulder and looked up. It was his father.

'You enjoy yourself tonight, son. You have fun and dance. William'll be watching you tonight, I'm sure, and he'll want to see you laughing.'

John looked around, half expecting to see William leap out from behind the fires built up on the big common field. After all, that's what they'd be watching for tonight. Ghosts. On Midsummer's Eve, the eve of the Feast of St John, the spirits could enter this world. The fires would be lit to keep them away. There were three fires: the fire of clean bones whose stench would frighten the spirits, the wake-fire of wood to light the night for the watchers, and the bone and wood fire dedicated to St John – John's own patron saint – who had baptised Jesus. The fires would hold the spirits away, wouldn't they? And Midsummer's Night wasn't very long, was it?

'Come on, John!'

Here were Ralph, Alan and Henry, – his and William's best friends. It was nearly dusk. Before the vigil they had other things to do.

The four of them made their way over to the beech woods at Box where the rest of the folk of Minchinhampton were gathered. There, held up by Robert Benet the smith and Richard Bigg the wheelwright, was the wheel. John and his mates had helped cover the wheel with straw earlier, and it was their job to set it rolling down the hill. John gulped as he looked at the wheel with its two rods sticking out on either side. He gulped again as he looked at the assembled people of the manor. If the wheel rolled down to the stream the sun would shine all summer and there would be a good harvest. If the wheel fell before it got there the harvest would be bad.

'Let's do it,' John said.

The four lads led the wheel to the edge of the hill where men with flaming torches waited. The sun was like a torch in the sky, low and golden. People were shouting. John placed himself by one of the rods, ready to guide the wheel. It was a long way down the hill and the way wasn't smooth. The wheel would dance over tussocks and bushes and rocks on its way to the stream.

If it got that far.

The crowd fell silent as the men with torches approached the wheel. John saw Ralph brace himself. Henry was grinning. Alan looked solemn.

The torch touched the straw, and with a 'whumph' the flames took, and they were off, rolling the wheel downhill, the burning straw like a furnace beside them, feet stumbling as they raced down, Ralph whooping. With one hard push they let the wheel go – and go it did! It was flying, it was bounding, streaks of fire shooting out, and John was running. Look at it go! Surely it would reach the stream and give them the harvest they needed? Henry tripped and rolled, only to spring up, laughing. Other young men were following them. The wheel bounded down and down into the

trees. Just after it disappeared John heard a splash.

The four of them hauled the sopping, broken pieces back to the top of the hill in triumph. Then the party started in earnest. There was free bread, meat and cider. As soon as the three fires were lit, the piper and drummer struck up a tune and the dancing began. John flung himself into the dance as the sun finally set. Round and round the fire they wove. He'd never danced like this before, leaping and hopping high.

They danced for hours, until the music stopped and those who didn't have to keep the vigil began to leave. In the fires' flickering light John saw someone coming towards him. Alice de Wite, fourteen like him, baptised the same day. She looked lovely in the firelight and he felt a blush rising up his cheeks.

'I picked you a rowan twig.' She handed him a slender, smoothed-down stick. 'You'll need it – to protect you from the spirits … if you want it?'

He opened his mouth but no sound came out.

Her face fell.

'I do!' He quickly took the stick and tied it into his shirt. 'Um, thank you.'

She smiled, craned over, and pecked his cheek. With a laugh she was gone.

John stood there a long time, his cheek burning.

He turned back to the wake-fire. This was it! It was St John's Eve and the spirits were out there. Alan waved him over to the lads and they were instantly on to him about Alice. But their laughter soon died away as the quiet of the night settled on the men keeping vigil. They strained their eyes into the darkness, looking out for spirits.

'They say Mogga, the beast of the moor, also roams tonight,' whispered Alan, and they all shivered.

'I heard that old Sercherman's uncle once went to the church on St John's Eve,' said Ralph in a hushed voice. 'They say that you can see in church then who's to die that year – and he saw himself! He was dead when they found him next morning.'

John felt the blood drain from his cheeks. If he'd gone to the church last year would he have seen William?

Henry gave Ralph a nudge.

'Sorry,' muttered Ralph. 'We miss him, too.'

'Do you think—' John flung his hand towards the darkness, wanting to ask if they thought William was out there tonight, with the spirits, but the words wouldn't come.

Alan shook his head. 'The fires are burning. So the spirits can't come.'

'And you've got your twig!' cried Henry, and they all laughed again.

The chatter of the little groups of men died away to a comfortable silence as the darkness deepened. The night dragged on. John stared into the darkness, remembering his brother and the good times they'd had.

At length he heard a movement, and looked up. The sky was a pre-dawn grey. His friends were getting up to go. The fires had burnt themselves out. Henry cocked his head, inviting John to follow, but John shook his head. He wanted one more moment. His fingers found the rowan twig and he pulled it from his shirt with a smile, then he turned to look out at the flat expanse of the misty common field. St John's Day – and a good harvest to follow, as the wheel had gone into the stream.

From the corner of his eye he caught a movement. By the edge of the wood stood a misty figure. He could barely see it, but his heart began to thump. The figure raised a hand as if in farewell. As the dawn's light washed over the hill, the faint form faded away.

15

YUBBERTON YAWNIES

It was time for the Cotswolds Best Church Tower competition, and everyone in Ebrington knew that Chipping Campden was going to win it yet again. They always won it, and no wonder! Their church tower was tall and straight with four storeys and fancy finials.

Ebrington's tower was short and squat with only two storeys and hardly any finials. But it did sit on a hill. There was a fine view from it – except that you could see straight down to Campden and its tower. Ebrington folk did what they could to beautify their tower. They scrubbed it clean and put out flowers, but the judges would surely vote for the fancier church!

The villagers knew they had to do something special. One day, when Sarah Southam was putting manure on her flowers, packing it round to make them grow and flourish, her husband Matthew was watching, and he had an idea …

That night at the Ebrington Arms he told the other men about it: 'Lads, let's gather up all the muck from all the farms. If it can grow my Sarah's petunias, it can grow the church!'

Everyone thought this was a brilliant idea. Round the farms they went with wheelbarrows, collecting muck. Whenever a horse and cart came through the village, the men were out with shovels and buckets and a hopeful look on their faces. They were usually lucky, as their staring made the horses get nervous!

Soon there was a steaming, stinking pile of manure mulching by the church on the hill. The reek made babies wail when they were christened, put people off their communion bread – why, the smell must've turned bodies in their coffins during funerals!

That Sunday all the men of the village – save Tommy Abbotts, who never did a day's work if he could help it – trooped to the church with their pitchforks. After the service, Matthew led them to the muckheap and they all plunged their pitchforks in and hoicked some well-rotted dung.

They mucked the church tower like Sarah's flowers. The muck covered the door and the windows above it, the men slathering it on and packing it in. Out came the ladders and they mucked the tower until the muck was as high as the church roof. It didn't half look strange, the church buried up to its ears in brown stinking dung!

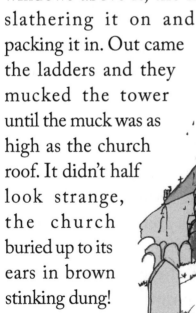

The men came back eagerly each day to look for signs the tower had started growing, but the reek soon sent them scuttling away. It smelt so bad that next Sunday the villagers all stamped down to Campden to attend the service there instead. Campden church tower was looking especially fine and tall, and its congregation seemed especially smug.

'Just let 'em wait,' the Ebrington folk muttered. 'They'll be laughing on the other side of their faces when we've growed our church and won the prize!'

When they got back they trooped up the path to their church to inspect the muck. They saw a brown stain on the stonework above the top of the manure.

'Look at that!' cried Matthew Southam. 'The tower do be a-growing! That be a whole foot taller than it were before!'

Every day the stain grew bigger. The tower was growing apace!

The day before the competition they cleared away all the muck and the women set to cleaning the stonework till the whole church sparkled. The aroma of the muck lingered, though, so they scattered rose water around the base of the tower.

Everyone was turned out in their Sunday best when the judges came. The tower might not have grown a new storey, but it surely did look taller! But the judges' noses were twitching. Their faces were growing red and they were holding their hands in front of their mouths.

'Don't you like our lovely tall new tower?' asked Matthew.

'Taller?' cried the judges. 'That tower's no taller than last year!'

The villagers stared at the tower and the truth began to dawn.

The tower hadn't grown.

All that had happened was that the muck had sunk.

As this sank in, one of the judges delicately asked, 'But – tell me, please, what is that rather curious smell? Like roses and, well, muck.'

Ebrington didn't win the competition. Not even a 'commended'! Once more Campden carried away the prize. Ebrington folk could hardly bear to go down to Campden because the people there were so smug. So they planted a line of trees on their hill so they could no longer see Campden church.

The memory of the defeat lingered in folk's minds all that year, just as a faint whiff of manure lingered at the church. When the time for the church tower contest came round again, the women banned the men from trying anything.

'We'll just make it as beautiful as we can, with cleaning and flowers and decoration.'

The vicar's wife even made people take off their shoes before going in the church in case a speck of muck got in.

'It'll certainly be the best *kept* tower,' muttered Matthew to his neighbour, Charlie Green, as he levered his boots back on after a service.

The night before the competition the men were once more in the Ebrington

Arms. Over glasses of ale they grumbled they'd not be able to show their faces in Chipping Campden if Campden won the prize again.

Matthew said, 'The trouble be, the church ben't in the roight spot. That tower'd be taller if twur higher up the hill!'

The men all exchanged a look.

'We'll go up there an' move him then!' cried Charlie. He called for the landlord to give them bread and cheese to fortify them, and another glass to steady their nerves.

It was a warm summer's evening. When they'd trooped up to the church, they pulled off their jackets and flung them in a pile on the north side of the tower so they weren't in the way. No one noticed Tommy Abbotts creep away.

Then they marched round to the south side and set their shoulders against the wall.

'Roight-ho, butties!' cried Matthew. 'When I says "Heave", heave!'

So they heaved and pushed against the tower. While they were doing this, Tommy

Abbotts snuck back to the heap of jackets – and for a lark he carried them all away!

On the other side of the tower the men were still pushing – till Matthew cried, 'All roight, that should've done it!'

They hurried round to see how far up the hill they'd pushed the tower. But something was missing. Where were their jackets?

'Look at that!' cried Charlie Green. 'We've gone and moved the tower on to our jackets!'

They said not a word to their wives. The next day the judges came. They took in the sparkling church, the shining bells, the mass of glorious flowers, and went into a whispering huddle.

Ebrington won the prize!

The judges said they'd never seen a cleaner, fresher tower. Size wasn't everything, after all. The women preened at their words, but the men silently smirked at each other. They knew the real reason why they'd won. It was because they'd moved the tower and it truly was higher!

16

HARVEST HOME

The last day of the harvest! Tonight Farmer Hartland would lay out a fine feast in thanks for everyone's hard work. Fred Iles was worried, though. He'd overheard the farmer talking to his wife: 'The harvest's a thin one this year. It'll be a lean old winter.' It was only Fred's second time as a reaper. As he swung his sickle over and over, the corn seemed to go on for miles. But what did he know?

By mid-afternoon they were at the furthest corner of the field. Just one sheaf to go. With great ceremony old Dobbs tied the last standing corn into four bunches so it was like a horse lying upside down. Fred felt a frisson of excitement. If he could catch the Mare he'd be Harvest Lord!

They all gathered round, and to shouts and jests the first reaper turned his back on the sheaf and hurled his sickle over his shoulder. Fred jeered with the rest as it sailed straight over the Mare. It wasn't so funny when it was his turn. A bead of sweat trickled down his neck. No way to take aim; you just had to throw. As soon as the sickle left his hand he knew from the men's groans that it hadn't made its mark. Never mind. Not one of them even grazed the Mare first time round.

Second go – there was a gasp when Fred's sickle flew. For a moment he thought he'd done it. But no. In the end, it was Todd Workman who cut the last sheaf. Of course. Todd, the farm's golden boy. Todd who was courting Polly Webb, the Harvest Queen.

Fred sighed and took a long draw of cider as Todd cried out, 'I 'ave her, I 'ave her, I 'ave her!' Fred's calling of 'What hast thee?' was lacklustre, but Todd was jubilant as he cried out, 'A Mare!'

With deft fingers old Dobbs coiled the stalks of the Mare to make the corn dolly. Todd carried it in triumph to the wagon. Fred's heart sank as Polly came running into the field to greet her Harvest Lord.

She was a sight for sore eyes, their Harvest Queen. Dressed up in a fine white linen gown tied with a yellow sash. The straw hat over her yellow hair festooned with flowers. She solemnly took the Mare from Todd and clambered on to the wagon to install it in pride of place at the front of load. The wagon and the horses were as fancy as she, bedecked with flowers and scarlet ribbons. The children sprawling on top were tricked out in their Sunday best. It was a fine show, but Fred felt sour as he watched Todd whispering to Polly.

He turned away to take his place with the other reapers – then suddenly Polly was there beside him.

'No long face today, Fred Iles! 'Tis Harvest Home and soon we'll be a-feasting.'

Fred hated her in that moment, but then she said, 'Todd said you threw well today. He reckons as you'll get it next year.'

Somewhat mollified, Fred fell in beside the wagon. Todd jumped on to it to steer the horses, Polly mounted Mistress Hartland's white pony, and they were off! Fred raised his voice with the rest as they sang the old songs and passed around the remaining cider keg.

Soon Farmer Hartland's house hove into view. Once they were in the farmyard, Todd leapt down off the cart and, as he did every year, climbed on to a shed roof and in his fine voice cried out:

> *We have ploughed, we have sowed,*
> *We have reaped, we have mowed,*
> *We have brought home every load,*
> *Hip, hip, hip, Harvest Home!*

All the workers on the farm spilled out, and Farmer Hartland with them, belly straining against his yellow waistcoat, raising the 'Huzzah!' in reply. Mistress Hartland welcomed them into the barn, where cakes and more cider were waiting to ease their hunger and thirst before the feast began.

Young Sukey, her daughter, handed Fred a cup with a simpering smile, and Fred gulped it straight down.

Soon enough he was feeling the effects of that cider and he slipped out of the barn to have a wee. Coming back, he heard the laughter and chatter from the barn. He hesitated. It was very pleasant to be alone, and quiet. He closed his eyes and felt the warmth of the last of the day's sun on his face. Savoury aromas from the brewhouse nearby wafted past his nose.

Today the brewhouse was given over to cooking the food for the feast. The smells drew Fred over. He peeked through a gap in the slatted walls – and saw something terrible.

Farmer Hartland was bending over a vat of stew. As Fred watched, the farmer dropped in an old leather boot and stirred it in! Fred was astounded. Was the harvest so bad they had to be fed old boots? What should he do? Farmer Hartland was the boss. If Fred spoke out he'd surely lose his job and then where would he be?

He slowly made his way back to the barn. After more cake and cider he managed to push what he'd seen to the back of his mind. The day wore into night and the farm workers started bringing in the feast. That image of the boot splashing into the stew wouldn't go away.

In came the goose and the puddings and pies, each dish raising a cheer. Fred knew he should speak but couldn't bring himself to do it. He saw Polly and Todd looking at him askance. They'd be thinking he was still smarting at not being Harvest Lord. He wished that he dared tell them the truth.

Then Farmer Hartland and a lad brought in the steaming vat of stew and placed it centre stage. Todd stood up and began to declaim again, this time praising the farmer: 'Here's a health unto our master …'

Some master! Who wants a master who feeds you old boots? But Fred still didn't dare speak. Maybe he should simply keep quiet and not eat the stew?

When Sukey started ladling out the stew he could stand it no longer.

He jumped to his feet. 'Don't eat it! It's got Farmer Hartland's old boots in it!'

There was immediate uproar. Sukey and the Mistress cried out denials, but Farmer Hartland looked shifty. Polly ran to the pot and rootled about with the ladle. Everyone fell silent. You could've heard a pin drop. Slowly Polly lifted a long, snaky thing from the stew.

A bootlace!

Mistress Hartland rounded on her husband with a furious yell and he fled from the barn. Everyone erupted in laughter. The Mistress shouted at Sukey to fetch their own fine hams kept for the winter.

When the hubbub died down, all eyes fell on Fred. Todd walked over to him and raised Fred's arm as if he were a champion.

'Well, Fred's done us a fine service tonight.'

Everyone laughed again. Fred's face went red. Couldn't Todd just leave him alone?

But Todd hadn't finished. 'Now, now, everyone. We know it's been a thin harvest, but if we stick together and help each other we'll get through the winter. Let Fred be Harvest Lord alongside me. Let him be the one to pin up the Mare in the barn to keep us safe till next harvest.'

Polly called out, 'A cheer for Fred! Hip, hip, hip—'

Fred felt a grin spreading over his face. When the 'Huzzah!' came it was loud enough to lift the rafters.

17

THE FLAXLEY HARE

Molly Morgan's parents were both dead, so she was raising her brothers and sisters alone. It was hard work, keeping bellies fed and keeping her great-grandfather's old timber-framed house in Flaxley standing. There was a vegetable plot behind the house, and once a week Molly would take some of the veg to market in Gloucester. It was ten miles and more, so she had to set off long before sunrise to get a good pitch. Otherwise her veg wouldn't sell! Yawning, she'd clamber out of bed, hoick the laden panniers on to her patient donkey, and set off down the road in darkness.

That morning, the moon still high in the sky, she was passing through Westbury when she heard something that made her stop dead. It had sounded for all the world like a hunting horn! There, in the Squire's big pasture, a hare was racing around in circles, as they do, kicking up so much dew that the animal shone in the moonlight.

The hare looped closer and closer to Molly, and then, quick as a flash, was on the wall beside her. It caught her gaze with its big brown eyes, and she saw that it was terrified. Then, with a bound, it leapt into one of her donkey's panniers!

Molly had never seen the like. But a hare would fetch a pretty penny at market.

She was just reaching to grab it when the hare spoke! 'Cover I wi' a napkin and don't think o' selling me! If twurn't for I, Molly Morgan, thy father'd never bin born!'

Then she heard that horn again. The hare gave a squeal and suddenly Molly's mind was made up.

'I'll protect ee,' she whispered, covering the hare with a cloth. 'God be my witness should I go agen my word!'

The horn sounded again. Out of thin air spilled dozens of mounted huntsmen decked out in scarlet. Coal-black hounds with burning red eyes raced beside them.

The leader of the hunt rode up and asked Molly in rich folks' plummy tones if she'd seen a hare go past.

Molly stared. The man's skin was beet red – and were those *horns* under his cap?

'No hares've a-passed by,' she said.

The huntsman slung his cap to the ground and Molly saw he was indeed the Devil!

'We've lost the scent, lads!' he cried. 'Now git – before the cock crows!'

Off they raced, the hounds' black tails wagging as they leapt back into the air.

'I thank ee,' said the hare. 'Thouse a-broke the curse on me! In life I was once a maid as fresh as thee, but when I died, acoz I were a witch, I was cursed to be coursed by the Devil till he catched me – or till I saw the tails on all his hounds afore the cock crowed in the morning. Now I seen them! I will be free!'

The hare made to bound away, but Molly was quick. 'Wait a minute! Free you may be, but you owe me some explaining. What did you mean "my father might never bin born"?'

The hare gave her a long look. 'Weren't there no tales o' hares in thy family?'

Molly went cold. Hadn't there been a silly story about her grandpa wooing her granny as a hare?

'You mean – that do be true?'

The hare laughed. 'As true as thee dost live and breathe, Molly Morgan! Thy gaffer was a Welshman, and thy great-grandpa didn't think much on him. Banned him from seeing thy granny, he did. But thy gaffer, he loved thy granny, and he weren't having it, so he came to me. I was an awld biddy then and I had the knowing o' things. I learned him a thing or two about watching the hares – how they move, how they see, what they do, and I showed him how to get in their minds …'

'You mean …?'

'One Sunday, thy great-grandpa was outside that old house o' his and he seed thy gaffer a-walking up the road towards the church as was there afore they built that fine new one. He was grizzled to see thy gaffer gie him a cheery wave! He zed nothing, an' soon enough thy gaffer was out o' sight.

'But then, guess what? A hare sprang up on the high bank behind the house, staring down into the garden where thy granny were fetching water. Thy great-grandpa, he *knew*. He got his gun and he shot that hare!

'It got all round Flaxley as young Morgan was hurted. Thy granny, she knew what'd happened. Her went to her father and told him if he wunt back down she'd away to Wales wi' her man!

'Well, back down he did – an' thee dost live yet in that old house!'

Molly could hardly believe this mad tale. But she was listening to a talking hare telling it, so maybe she was mad as well!

The cock crowed.

'Free!' cried the hare. She leapt from the panniers, over the wall, back into the field.

As Molly watched, the hare started to run round and round and a light began to shimmer above the centre of the field. As the light grew, Molly saw through it a place very different from the dark pasture – a sunny, flower-filled meadow, with a bluebell wood beyond.

The hare ran through the light into the meadow and, as she did, was transformed into a young woman barely older than Molly.

'I'll send ee good luck from where I be a-wending to,' the woman cried.

With that, the woman, the meadow, the wood, and the light were gone. Molly and her donkey were left standing on the road in the darkness.

She was late to market that day, but, strangely, the best pitch hadn't gone. Her veg sold well, and quickly. After that, her plot of land prospered, giving out more than she put in. She was able to buy a cart for market day, to buy in some help with the land and her brothers and sisters, and to fix up the old house. Before she knew it, her family was rich!

Molly never said what'd happened that
morning, not even when she was a granny
herself. She never let anyone hurt a hare.
Sometimes she'd slip into the fields to watch
them and wonder how it felt to run as one.
But if she found out, she wasn't telling.

18

THE TAILOR OF GLOUCESTER

It was an especially busy time at Prichard the tailor's in St John's Lane, just behind the Cathedral. John Prichard and his pair of young assistants could tailor you a shirt, jacket, or trousers, a petticoat, gown, or corset. You name it and they could make it. But now the leaves were turning brown and falling from the trees, and everyone who was anyone was getting ready for the Gloucestershire Root, Fruit & Grain Society's annual show. On 9 November – the same date each year – all the councillors, all the farmers from miles around, would

process through the streets of Gloucester to
Shire Hall. For this and the judging of the
show and the splendid dinner afterwards,
they would be dressed in their best. So John
Prichard was flooded with orders for fine
clothes that needed making or mending.

One particular order was more important
than any other. This year there was a new
mayor. He wanted a fancy new waistcoat
for the occasion and John was determined
to make him the finest you could imagine.
It would be made of peach-coloured silk
embroidered with rosebuds, and stitched
along the seams with silver and gold thread.
John was so busy, so keen to impress the
Mayor – and he couldn't trust those young
assistants with something so special – that
he had to ask a couple of the councillors if
they could manage without new waistcoats
this year.

By Saturday afternoon, just a few days till
the show, John had measured and cut all the
pieces of silk needed to make the Mayor's
waistcoat. He laid them out on the table

together with the pocket flaps, the buttons, the lengths of silver and gold thread, and a skein of cherry-coloured 'twist' – twisted silk with which to stitch the buttonholes. Everything was ready to make up the waistcoat on Monday. Then he locked up the shop, pocketed the key, and went home to his mum and dad, with whom he lived – and with whom he had to go to church on Sunday.

Later than Saturday evening, much later, some hours after dark, John Prichard's two assistants came staggering to the shop in St John's Lane. They'd been enjoying some cider at the New Inn and were feeling too tired and sleepy to walk all the way to their own homes. The tailor's shop was much nearer. They luckily had with them a key to the door. So they let themselves in. They were too sleepy to notice the materials John had laid out for the Mayor's waistcoat. Amidst the clutter of the shop – the workbenches, sewing machine, and steam press, the rolls of fabric and reels of thread, the mirrors and tape measures and needles and scissors – the two lads lay down on the floor and went to sleep.

You know what it's like when you sleep in an unusual place? You have strange dreams. You keep waking up and wondering where you are. It had been a long week at work and a long evening at the pub. The two young men were still sleeping and dreaming long after the autumn sunshine began to peek through the crack between the curtains. When they did wake up, they felt pretty rough. They had no razor to shave their chins, no comb to tidy their tousled hair, and their clothes were smelly because they'd worn them all night. They couldn't be seen outside in such a state on a Sunday morning. And they were still so tired. They pulled the curtains closer and went back to sleep. In muddled moments of waking they heard scuffles and squeaks around them, and footsteps and voices in the lane. Through their eyelids the light sometimes brightened as when a cloud slips from the sun. They dreamt of people they'd never seen and places they'd never been.

Sometime in the afternoon, when they were awake, they found in the cupboard some cheese and dry bread and half a bottle of wine. They still dared not go outside. They chatted and found ways to pass the time and then slept and snored some more.

Only at dusk did they at last sneak out. They locked the door behind them, shook hands as old friends with a shared secret, and ambled away through the gaslit streets to their homes.

First thing Monday morning, John Prichard arrived at his shop, all spruced and shaven, ready to resume work on the Mayor's waistcoat. He'd have it half made, he reckoned, by the time those two scallywags, his assistants, turned up for work. But when he unlocked the door and stepped inside, what was the first thing he saw? Right there on the table – the Mayor's waistcoat already finished! The pieces sewn together, the pockets attached, the seams worked in silver and gold, and the buttonholes stitched with cherry twist – all save the last one. Pinned beside that unfinished buttonhole was a scrap of paper on which were scrawled the words 'No more twist'.

How could this be? Who could possibly have got into the shop and done the job since John left on Saturday? There was only one explanation: it must have been the fairies! There were still a few of them about in Gloucester, people said. Only the fairies could have passed through locked-up doors and windows and accomplished such a fine job on a Sunday, when no respectable man or woman should be working. A fine job it was too – as neatly done as John would have done it himself.

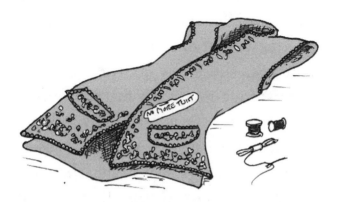

It took just a jiffy, once he'd bought some more twist, to finish the last buttonhole. The Mayor's new waistcoat was ready! But the Mayor didn't need it just yet. There were still a few days till the show. So John displayed the garment in his shop window, and beside it a sign saying:

COME TO PRICHARD WHERE THE WAISTCOATS
ARE MADE AT NIGHT BY THE FAIRIES

It was quite a mystery, but you have to make the best of these things. John was running a business after all. Maybe the waistcoat and sign in the window did help to bring in some extra customers once the flurry of work for the annual show was over. But better was yet to come.

You see, the story of the tailor and the waistcoat made by fairies came to the attention of a writer called Beatrix Potter, who was staying with her cousin at Harescombe Grange near Edge. Miss Potter thought it such a good story that she wrote her own version of it. Only she made a few changes from what really happened. She set the tale at Christmas, made the tailor an old man with a cat, and replaced the fairies with mice. She published the story as a picture book called *The Tailor of Gloucester* and it sold very well. It sold so well that the real tailor, John Prichard, got so many orders for clothes that there was never a moment of slack. There was plenty of work for his two assistants, who said not a word about it; just kept their heads down and their fingers nimble and got on with the work.

In time John Prichard became quite well-to-do. He got married – twice – and had four children and moved to a nice house in Thornbury and later to Cheltenham. When he died, in 1934, he was buried in Charlton Kings. On his gravestone are the words:

THE TAILOR OF GLOUCESTER

19

OWLPEN MANOR

David knew he was going to hate Owlpen Manor as soon as the bus left Stroud. Stroud was a stupid little town, but the bare hills outside it were worse. The bus drove up into thick fog on top of the hills and then out of the fog into another world, all steep hills and tall trees. David's tummy lurched at the sheer drops as the bus skidded down towards a village. Waiting for them outside the pub was a horse and cart. A real horse, like the rag-and-bone man had. The other kids were excited, nudging each other and talking too loudly. They ignored David. They'd ignored him since they'd all piled on the train at Paddington and he'd got out his book. They'd all stared as if they'd never seen a book before. David was used to being the odd one out. He didn't care.

They didn't see the manor house until they were there. It was in the middle of nowhere. And so old! David couldn't see a single other house. It made him, a city boy, feel weird. They were ushered into the house and sat down on uncomfortable old chairs. A stern woman gave them a lecture, full of rules. As evacuees, they were to go to school in the village, but they had to do their bit for the war by helping with the vegetables. They weren't to disturb the lady of the house, Mrs Bray. And no complaining. After all, wasn't there a war on? David really hated Hitler then. First Hitler had made his dad go and fight, then he'd bombed London so David had to come to this stupid old house, and now he had to dig vegetables!

He and the other three boys were shown the room where they were to sleep. Then everyone trooped down another staircase for tea, or 'dinner' as they called it here. It was good, with cheese and cream and meat!

Not like at home. Maybe they didn't have rationing in the countryside? On the way back up from tea David spotted a big white owl above a door. When he looked away from the owl, the other boys were gone. He had no idea which way to go, so he ran up the first staircase he saw. Phew – he recognised where he was, but as he started along the corridor the hairs rose on the back of his neck. He was being watched!

He turned – and at the top of the stairs was a sight that took his breath away. A woman stood there, dressed in exactly the kind of clothes someone who owned a place like this should wear – a long dress with a tight, fur-trimmed top half and really full skirts. And her hat! It was amazing – sort of tall and folded over itself with gauzy fabric to either side. She was looking right at him. David realised his mouth was wide open. He shut it with a snap. This must be Mrs Bray! She seemed to look right through him, but then gave him a gentle smile before drifting off down the stairs. Hmm, maybe Owlpen wouldn't be too bad if people dressed like that all the time!

Of course, they didn't. The gardeners wore heavy coats and hobnail boots. Cook and the housekeeper wore black. Occasionally he saw a woman in a tweedy knee-length skirt who people said was Mrs Bray. She didn't look anything like his lady, but maybe it was just the different clothes. School started, and it was horrible. The kids there hated the evacuees, the evacuees hated them, and everyone hated David. Free time was spent digging up potatoes. The local people talked funny. David finished the books he'd brought. He'd seen a big library in the house, but didn't dare go in there. He missed his mum and dad so much it made his tummy ache. And sometimes, when he was alone, it felt like there were people in the house watching him.

That Christmas all David wanted to do was go home. Mrs Bray must have known that they all did, because it was announced that there was to be a party. Boxes were brought down from the attic to a big bedroom with painted cloths with trees and animals on them. They were full of old clothes, spangly fabric and papier mâché crowns. For once the other kids let David play with them. They had fun trying on the clothes. Cook even rustled up a cake with real cocoa powder in it! Then a figure in a long dress and a crown swept in. It was Mrs Bray in a fine dress again at last! She looked very nice, so David plucked up the courage to say so. 'The dress you wore the first evening was even better,' he added.

When he saw the look of shock on her face, his heart sank. He was in trouble now!

She sat him down on the bed and peppered him with questions about what he'd seen, what she'd worn, and where he'd seen her. He thought she looked rather grim when he'd told her, but she didn't tell him off. In fact, she started asking him other questions and, while the other kids played, he told her about missing his mum and dad, running out of books, how the others didn't like him and everything. She seemed pretty cross after all that, but she didn't say anything.

After Christmas, David had some surprises. First the other boys started to invite him to join in their games. Second, someone left a parcel of books on his bed. Third and best of all, just after New Year his dad turned up on his way to join a ship at Bristol. He'd managed to get a few hours' leave to see David, who dragged him all over the house, showing him those funny painted cloths, the plaster owl, the huge yew hedges where you could hide, the gardens given over to the veg they ate. It was a golden day. David was grinning as he waved his dad off.

He felt a bit hollow afterwards, as if the war he'd sort of forgotten about had come to Gloucestershire. Still, he had his new books. The one on top had a message inside from Mrs Bray: 'I think you might like this one.' It had a knight in armour on the cover and was about the War of the Roses. David sighed. He wasn't sure he wanted to read about another war, even if it was hundreds of years ago in the Middle Ages with kings and queens and knights. Mrs Bray had left a bookmark in it. He opened the book at that page – and there was a picture of a lady dressed just like *his* lady! He read the caption: 'Queen Margaret of Anjou before the Battle of Tewkesbury, 1471.'

Tewkesbury was in Gloucestershire, wasn't it? He read on. Margaret, the old queen, was fighting, with her son, Edward, against the new king, Edward IV. Then a word leapt off the page. *Owlpen*! Margaret had actually stayed right here the night before the battle! He read how her army marched north, then Edward IV's army had cut them off at the River Severn and they'd had to fight. Margaret's son was killed. He was seventeen, six years older than David. He had a sudden vision of his own mum waving him off to war with tears streaking her face. Margaret had been captured, he read. But it didn't say what she'd felt about her son dying.

He thought of the lady he'd seen and suddenly it made sense. This must have been the last place Margaret had felt happy. She was still here, remembering when her son was still alive and there was hope. That's what Mrs Bray was trying to tell him. David put the book away and picked up the next book, an adventure story. He'd had enough of war.

The weeks passed. Now the other kids were becoming his friends, things were better. David tried to put Queen Margaret out of his head. Then one day in February he suddenly felt really odd. He hadn't been missing his mum so much, but now he really wanted to see her. He had a fluttery, sick feeling inside. He knew that he had to go home. It was important. He didn't know why, but it was.

He counted his pocket money, sneaked to the kitchen and grabbed some bread and cheese, then bolted out through the churchyard to the road to Uley. He hadn't got far when one of the farmhands spotted him and marched him back. David was furious. That sick feeling in his stomach was worse and he felt shaky. He knew he had to get to London. As soon as the coast was clear he shot off again. When they brought him back a third time, Mrs Bray sat him down and asked him why he was doing this. David didn't know why. Except he was sure his mum needed him. To his shame he began to cry.

They kept a close eye on him after that. He lay awake all night, determined to sneak out at the first glimmer of light. But as he was getting up he heard the ring of a bicycle bell and a knocking on the door. Hardly breathing, his heart thumping, David lay still. He knew that this was to do with him.

Sure enough, the bedroom door creaked open and someone shook him and led him down to where Mrs Bray was waiting in her dressing gown. Very gently indeed she told him that a telegram had come for him.

With trembling hands, he opened it. It was from his mum and very short: 'Dad lost in action. Coming on 6 o'clock train.'

Everyone was very sympathetic. Cook made cocoa and gave him cake for breakfast, but David couldn't eat. He felt numb. He could see his dad's cheery face as he waved goodbye last month. How could he be gone?

When everyone was eating lunch he sneaked upstairs. Something drew him to the room with the painted cloths. When he opened the door, there she stood, looking out of the window. Queen Margaret. She was transparent in the sunshine. He told her what had happened. He knew how she felt, lingering here. If only he could go back to that one golden day here with his dad, he would. She turned and gave him that gentle smile again, as if she understood. Then she faded away.

20

A NEW YEAR'S BLESSING

Tomorrow was New Year's Day and Grace Barlow wanted to make a pretty calend egg so they could beg coins and food to help them through till spring. The apple that little Joseph had fetched down from the loft was big and red with no sign of rot. He was supposed to help his mother decorate it, but now his dad was gone he was too great a man for such things, even though he was only eight. So Grace did it herself: the apple for *sweetness*, decorated with hazelnuts for *prosperity* and a sprig of yew for *long life* – the three gifts of the

Wise Men – and the whole thing perched on three sticks of holly wood.

It took them all day to tramp around the parish's five hamlets. Grace kept a solemn face; she had to look the part of the grieving widow and it unnerved her to go into folk's parlours and be watched by the men. Yet she tried to recite the words warmly when Joseph had put the calend egg on the table:

'Tis New Year's day and may ye be blessed
and may ye look kindly on this lowly guest.
Sweetness, health, and wealth
and God bless you well.
An apple, cheese, or penny
and God send you farewell.

The haul wasn't as much as she'd hoped. Times were getting harder for everyone. Life had been hard enough before Lewis passed away, but it had been much tougher since without his ploughman's wages. However hard Grace toiled, milking cows, picking apples, mending clothes, working her own strip of land, there was never quite enough. Often Joseph complained he was hungry.

Just a couple of days later, the hogglers came. It was already dark when Grace heard the commotion outside: the tuneless song, the shouts and laughter. She prayed they'd pass by her humble hovel – but no, *blam blam* on the door, and in they trooped. Joseph gasped and ran to hide behind his mum. Crowding into the little room, the men seemed gigantic in their tatters of cowhide and the sprays of box and holly sprouting from their heads. You could smell the earth on their faces and the cider on their breath. They might look like woodwoses, but Grace knew well enough who they were, including their leader – Edward Price, the churchwarden.

They sang two verses of their hoggling song, so raucous you couldn't make out the words. Then Master Price flourished a cap.

'Your contribution to the parish, Mistress Barlow!'

It made her so angry. 'Ye know we have nothing, not since my Lewis passed on.'

'Hard times come to many. Everyone must pay their fair share.'

The hogglers waited. They had a brooding, bustling energy. They were not their normal selves. You didn't know what they might do.

With a sigh, Grace stomped upstairs, Joseph scampering close behind her. She pulled from its hiding place her meagre bag of coins. Would a penny be enough to make the hogglers go? She took two.

Master Price emptied the coins with a clang on to the pewter plate held by David Morgan. The hogglers looked at each other …

'Thank you kindly, Mistress Barlow.'

A third man wrote down the sum and the coins were clinked into the bag carried by a fourth.

At least she'd given them less than she'd got with the calend egg! Once they were gone, Joseph found his courage and wanted to see the procession. Wrapped in their woollen mantles, they joined the little crowd following the hogglers by lantern light.

Rich and poor, every farmhouse and cottage got visited.

At last they reached the manor house. The hogglers disappeared inside. You could hear the muffled noise of their singing. It went on and on. The lord and his lady were getting the full treatment. The people waiting outside stamped their feet and slapped their arms to keep warm.

At last the hogglers reappeared. A glitter of silver and gold on the plate.

In a loud voice David Morgan announced the sum.

Boos and jeers from the crowd.

'Be it enough?' cried Edward Price.

'NO!'

The hogglers trooped back inside. Another raucous song. Back out they came. The sum announced this time was greater.

'Be we happy now?'

There were a few cries of 'Nay!' but the rest were satisfied. Time now for the hogglers to do their stamping, thigh-slapping dance. Some of them had sunk so much cider they could barely stand, let alone dance, but the crowd clapped along, till at last the hogglers staggered with their plunder across to the church.

The gentry had paid a fair bit more than tuppence, so maybe there was some justice in this brigandage. Grace didn't know what happened to the money. No doubt the parish had expenses that had to be paid.

Then it was Twelfth Eve and folk were out in the field by the corn mill to bless the fields. Last year Lewis had been one of the twelve ploughmen who built the Apostles' Fires, and Grace had stayed at home with Joseph. This year Joseph wanted to go. Maybe it was right they should go in his father's memory.

What a sight were the twelve fires flashing in the darkness, the flames reflected in the millpond! Master Price and his fellows were there, wild men no more, in their ordinary winter clothes. Someone pressed a cup of cider in Grace's hand. Each of the ploughmen intoned the name of the apostle his fire stood for. When it got to 'Judas' everyone hissed and booed. The children raced forward – Joseph among them! – to stamp out the flames.

Next they lit the big Jesus fire waiting in front of the others. As the flames leapt, the curate called out, 'May the land be blessed and fruitful this coming year!'

They all said amen to that and quaffed a mouthful of cider. They called blessings on the barley, the turnips, the carrots, the cattle, sheep and pigs, and the health of his lordship. With each blessing they took another swig of cider. Grace's head was spinning by the time it was done and the ploughmen were studying how the fires were burning and what that portended for the year's harvest and how the seed should be set on Plough Monday. The Jesus fire burnt strong and bright. Grace prayed, O Lord have pity on us, that there shall be enough for me and my little son!

'When do we get the cake?' Joseph whispered.

Soon they'd go down to the corn mill, where the ploughmen would have their reward of cider and cakes soaked in cider. Before that, everyone had to take their lanterns into the orchard. The apple trees too must be blessed. Splashes of cider on the roots to shouts of 'Wassail!' God forbid the apple harvest should fail and the men run out of cider! Grace gave her cup to Joseph so he could splash the dregs of cider on the chosen tree. He jumped up and down, laughing, as if he'd done something naughty.

While Grace watched her son, a man appeared beside her. Edward Price.

'Christmas blessings to you, Mistress Barlow.' He dropped with a chink a little package into her hand. 'With the compliments of the parish.'

'But— ?'

'Say nothing of it. You're a widow now. The parish shall not let you and your lad starve in these lean months.'

Joseph scampered back and handed her the empty cup.

'Wassail!' he piped.

Yes, may God bless them all! Sweetness, health, and wealth! All the people of the parish. All the fields and their produce. And the trees in the orchards, so there'd be a fine crop of apples to hoard, and one especially big and red to make the calend egg to bring blessings next year too.

GLOSSARY

acoz	because
afore	before
agen	against
ain't	hasn't
alembic	round container with a long beak used by alchemists
a-mothering	going to celebrate Mothering Day
Apostles' Fires	set of bonfires that represent the twelve apostles
apothecary	person who sells medicines
a-wending	going
awld	old
ben't	isn't
bide	stay
bin	been
boy-chap	youth

butty	mate
calend egg	symbol of blessing made from an apple, sticks, nuts and herbs
Cavalier	wealthy Royalist in the English Civil War
chemise	woman's shirt-like undergarment
Christmastide	the season of Christmas
commons, common land	land used by the whole community
cotte	long dress or tunic
cromlech	prehistoric tomb made of large stones
Cupid	Roman god of love
doublet	short padded jacket
dryad	female tree spirit
ee	you
elixir	special potion
evacuee	child sent away from danger of bombing in the Second World War
finial	decorative feature on the top of a building
Flora	Roman goddess of spring
gaffer	grandad
grizzled	annoyed
gunwale	the top of the side of a boat

hoggler	member of group that collects donations for the parish
Lent	the season before Easter
lute	stringed instrument played by plucking
May Day	first day of May
Mothering Day	Sunday in the middle of Lent when families get together
nation	very
nigh	nearly
oultn't	will not
peel	shovel to take loaves in and out of the oven
Plough Monday	first day of ploughing in January
Plough Sunday	church festival in January to bless the land
Puritan	strict kind of Protestant Christian
punt	flat-bottomed boat pushed along with a pole
rationing	system to limit how much food everyone is allowed
seed	saw
simnel cake	fruitcake eaten during Lent
slabbered	dirty
tain't	it hasn't

telegram	early kind of text message sent along telegraph wires
Terpsichore	Greek goddess of dance
thouse	you have
trow	large flat-bottomed cargo boat
tush	pull
Twelfth Eve	the last evening of the twelve days of Christmas
twur	it were
twurn't	it weren't
Tyndale's Bible	translation of the Bible into English by William Tyndale
viol	stringed instrument played with a bow
wassail!	be healthy!
we'm	we are
Whitsun, Whitsuntide	the week's holiday including Whit Sunday
woodwose	legendary wild man of the woods
wunt	wouldn't
yawnie	silly person
yent	aren't
Yubberton	Ebrington
yur	here
zed	said

ACKNOWLEDGEMENTS

We wish to acknowledge the sources we've listed and the links in the chain by which the stories, customs and rhymes reached these sources. Wherever possible we've used multiple sources. For information and inspiration we're most grateful for help from Graham Bathe on 'A Midsummer Night's Watch', Caroline Lowsley-Williams at Chavenage House on 'The Candle in the Window', Jane Lund at Chipping Sodbury Library on 'The Immortal Cat of Chipping Sodbury', Mags Smith on 'Crocket's Hole', Jess Wilson on 'The Flaxley Hare', Lorraine Endersby of Brockweir and Hewelsfield History Group on 'The Mermaid's Curse', and Peter Wells (who's been instrumental in reviving the custom of the Apostles' Fires at Pauntley) on 'A New Year's Blessing'. Many thanks also to Martin Large and Meredith Debonnaire for sparking the idea that led to this book; to Nicola Guy and Ele Marr for making it happen; and to Fiona Eadie, Austin Keenan, Laura Kinnear, Alastair McNaught, Temi Odurinde, Chantelle Smith, Glenn and Mags Smith and Tim Willcocks for their attentive listening. Finally, a special thank you to Ele Marr for the beautiful cover art. All the other illustrations are by Kirsty.

SOURCES

Atkyns, R., *The Ancient and Present State of Glostershire* (R. Gosling, 1712)

Blunt, J.H., *Dursley and Its Neighbourhood* (Simpkin, Marshall, 1877)

Briggs, K., *A Dictionary of British Folk Tales in the English Language* (Indiana University Press, 1971)

Cheltenham Chronicle and Gloucestershire Graphic, 'The Sea Serpent of Coombe Hill', 16 January 1904

Drake, N., *The Plays and Poems of William Shakespeare, Vol. 1* (T. Cadell & W. Davies, 1817)

Grinsell, L.V. 'The Druid Stoke Megalithic Monument', *Transactions of the Bristol and Gloucestershire Archaeological Society*, Vol. 97 (1979)

Hare, K., *Gloucestershire* (Robert Hale, 1949)

Hartland, E.S., *Gloucestershire* (Folklore Society, 1895)

Hutton, R., *The Stations of the Sun* (Oxford University Press, 1996)

Kingshill, S. & Westwood, J., *The Fabled Coast* (Random House, 2012)

Leech, J., *Brief Romances from Bristol History* (William George, 1884)

Mander, N., 'The Ghosts of Owlpen', *Owlpen Manor Estate*, online

Matthews, R., *Haunted Gloucestershire* (Logaston Press, 2006)

Palmer, R., *The Folklore of Gloucestershire* (Westcountry Books, 1994)

Potter, B., *The Tailor of Gloucester* (Frederick Warne, 1969)

Ryder, T.A., *Gloucestershire Through the Ages* (Littlebury, 1950)

Thomas, R., 'Bristol – Legends, Pre-history and the Romans', *Ray's Miscellany*, online

Turner, M., *Mysterious Gloucestershire* (The History Press, 2011)

Westwood, J. & Simpson, J., *The Lore of the Land* (Penguin, 2006)

Williams, A., *Lays and Legends of Gloucestershire* (Kent, 1878)

Williams, A., *Round About the Upper Thames* (Duckworth, 1922)